Key Stage 3

Twentieth Century
British and World History
1900–2020

2nd edition

Laura Aitken-Burt and Robert Selth

William Collins' dream of knowledge for all began with the publication of his first book in 1819. A self-educated mill worker, he not only enriched millions of lives, but also founded a flourishing publishing house. Today, staying true to this spirit, Collins books are packed with inspiration, innovation and practical expertise.
They place you at the centre of a world of possibility and give you exactly what you need to explore it.

Collins. Freedom to teach.

Published by Collins
An imprint of HarperCollins*Publishers*
The News Building, 1 London Bridge Street, London, SE1 9GF, UK

HarperCollins*Publishers*
Macken House, 39/40 Mayor Street Upper, Dublin 1, DO1 C9W8, Ireland

Browse the complete Collins catalogue at
collins.co.uk

British Library Cataloguing-in-Publication Data
A catalogue record for this publication is available from the British Library.

Authors: Laura Aitken-Burt, Robert Selth
Series editor for Book 4: Robert Selth
Series editor: Robert Peal
Publisher: Katie Sergeant
Product manager: Joanna Ramsay
Editor: Caroline Low
Fact-checker: Barbara Hibbert
Proof-reader: David Hemsley
Cover designer: Gordon MacGilp
Cover image: Pictorial Press Ltd / Alamy Stock Photo
Typesetter: QBS
Production controller: Alhady Ali
Printed and bound by Martins the Printers

Acknowledgements
With thanks to Dr Kelly Hignett at Leeds Beckett University for review comments.
The publishers gratefully acknowledge the permission granted to reproduce the copyright material in this book. Every effort has been made to trace copyright holders and to obtain their permission for the use of copyright material. The publishers will gladly receive any information enabling them to rectify any error or omission at the first opportunity.

This book contains FSC™ certified paper and other controlled sources to ensure responsible forest management.

For more information visit: www.harpercollins.co.uk/green

Contents

UNIT 7: The Cold War

Enquiry Question: *Which superpower was more responsible for confrontations during the Cold War?*

UNIT 8: Civil Rights in the USA

Enquiry Question: *"The success of the Civil Rights Movement was due to the leadership of Martin Luther King." To what extent do you agree?*

UNIT 9: Decolonisation

Enquiry Question: *Why did most of Britain's colonies become independent during the 20th century?*

UNIT 10: Postwar Britain

Enquiry Question: *Has postwar Britain made life fairer for more people?*

Introduction

'As I write, highly civilised human beings are flying overhead, trying to kill me.'

George Orwell, 'England Your England', 1941

In the 20th century, the world was plunged into a chaotic whirlwind of violence, prejudice and fear. It was an era that saw death and destruction on a scale not previously even imagined. In many ways, this is a book about conflict – full of wars, revolutions and bitter hatreds between opposed groups of people.

The First World War was the original catastrophe: it created upheaval throughout Europe and led to the rise of brutal dictators all across the continent. These dictators then pushed the surviving democracies into a second and even greater world war.

Following the Second World War, the colonised people in Asia and Africa fought to win independence from their European rulers, while the greatest non-European power, China, entered a new era of its history. In what became the dominant nation in the world – the United States of America – there was a long struggle for justice before all its citizens could win equal legal rights. Even when the world wars were over, the international rivalry of the Cold War threatened to bring about still greater horrors, through the power of the nuclear bomb.

Robert Selth, co-author of Knowing History

Concise **chapter introductions** set the scene for each topic.

Fact boxes provide interesting, bite-sized information and details.

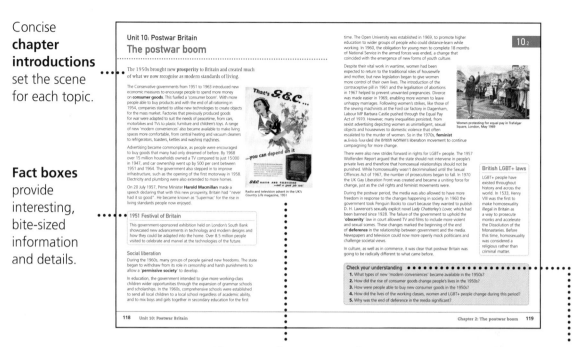

Photographs, maps and artwork illustrate and embed key concepts.

Check your understanding questions at the end of every chapter allow you to check and consolidate your learning.

Timelines map out the key dates from the unit, and help you understand the course of events. There is also a full timeline of events from across the units at the end of the book.

Knowledge organisers can be used to revise and quiz yourself on key dates, people and definitions.

Key vocabulary lists (in alphabetical order) at the end of each unit help you to find and define important terminology.

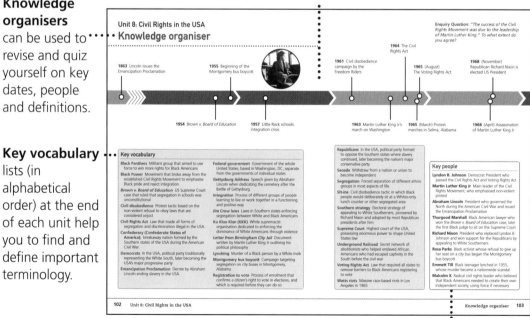

Key people lists (in alphabetical order) recap the people of influence covered in each unit.

Unit 1: The First World War
The outbreak of war

In June 1914, an isolated crisis in the south-east of Europe triggered a chain of responses that dragged all of Europe's major nations into war.

In the early 20th century, the five great powers of Europe – Britain, **Austria-Hungary**, Germany, France and Russia – existed in a **balance of power**, but fear and tension was growing between them. The great powers were divided into two opposed alliance systems:

- In 1882, Germany, Austria-Hungary and the less powerful nation of Italy had formed the **Triple Alliance**, a defensive pact that bound them to support each other in the event of war.
- In 1907, Britain, France and Russia formed a similar pact called the **Triple Entente** ('*entente*' is French for 'agreement'). These three nations were imperial rivals and regularly competed with each other for territory in Africa or Asia. However, all three nations also felt threatened by the rising power of Germany. Despite their rivalries overseas, they formed this alliance to protect themselves against German aggression in Europe.

Many people feared that the two groups of nations would end up at war. However, when war began, its trigger came from a very unexpected event.

The assassination of Franz Ferdinand

Austria-Hungary was a vast empire covering much of central and south-eastern Europe, which was ruled over by the Austrian emperor in Vienna. To the south, the empire bordered the small, independent nation of Serbia. Though relatively weak, Serbia had long been a source of trouble for Austria-Hungary. Many Serbian people lived in the southern provinces of the empire, and the main foreign policy of Serbia was to eventually 'liberate' those Serbs, breaking up Austria-Hungary and expanding Serbia by taking over the empire's southern territories. The Serbs therefore took every opportunity to irritate and destabilise the great power to their north.

On 28 June 1914, Archduke Franz Ferdinand, heir to the throne of Austria-Hungary, was visiting Sarajevo. This was a city in Bosnia, one of the southern provinces of the empire that contained a large population of Serbs. A Serbian terrorist group called the **Black Hand** seized this opportunity to try to assassinate the Archduke. The assassins failed on their first attempt: a bomb thrown at the Archduke's motorcade injured several people but did not harm Franz Ferdinand, who insisted on proceeding with his visit. However, while Franz Ferdinand was being driven to the city hospital to visit the wounded, a 19-year-old assassin named Gavrilo Princip successfully shot and killed him. The Archduke's wife, Sophie, was also killed.

Archduke Franz Ferdinand and his wife, Sophie, on the day they were assassinated

The July Crisis

The Austro-Hungarian government responded with shock and fury to the assassinations. It was immediately decided that they should invade Serbia, as punishment for the attack and in order to neutralise the Serbian threat once and for all. On 23 July, Austria-Hungary presented Serbia with an ultimatum demanding that Serbia meet a series of demands or face war. The Serbs refused, and on 28 July, Austria-Hungary declared war on Serbia.

So far, this was a war between one great power and one small nation. However, the Russian government, Serbia's traditional ally and protector, felt that they must come to Serbia's aid. On the evening of 30 July, Russia mobilised its army for war against Austria-Hungary. This put the German government in a very difficult position. Under the Triple Alliance, Germany was bound to go to war with Russia in order to defend its ally, Austria-Hungary. However, the Germans understood that war with Russia would also mean war with France and probably Britain. The Germans had long wished to avoid a situation where they would be forced to divide their armies to fight in both the west and the east at the same time. The **Schlieffen Plan** (see margin box) meant that when war came, Germany's first priority was to attack France as quickly and forcefully as possible.

On 1 August, Germany declared war against Russia. Two days later, it also declared war against France – and then immediately invaded. In order to attack France at the most convenient point, Germany chose to march the bulk of its armies through neutral Belgium. They entered Belgium on 4 August and faced immediate resistance from the Belgian army, as the tiny country refused to let German troops cross its territory. The violation of Belgian neutrality also prompted Britain to intervene, and so on 4 August, Britain declared war on Germany.

With the intervention of Britain, all five of the great powers were engaged, and Europe was at war. Britain, France and Russia became known as the Allies, while Germany and Austria-Hungary were called the **Central Powers**. Italy did not honour the Triple Alliance – instead, in 1915, it joined the war on the side of the Allies.

The Schlieffen Plan

To avoid fighting 'a war on two fronts' (with France to the west and Russia to the east), German war planning was based on the Schlieffen Plan. By this strategy, Germany would begin any war with a massive strike against France, allowing it to defeat France within six weeks. Only then would it shift most of its armies eastward to confront Russia.

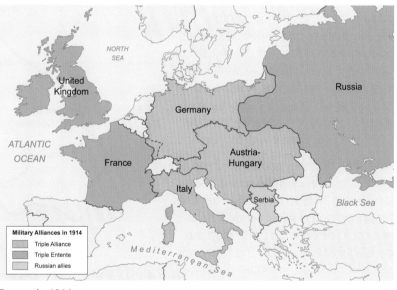

Europe in 1914

Check your understanding

1. How did Europe divide into two opposing alliances before 1914?
2. Why was Serbia such a problem for the Austro-Hungarian empire?
3. How did Austria-Hungary respond to the assassination of Franz Ferdinand on 28 June 1914?
4. What was the German war strategy laid out in the Schlieffen Plan?
5. Why did Britain enter the war on 4 August 1914?

Unit 1: The First World War
The Western Front

Much of the fighting in the First World War took place along a narrow strip of land in Belgium and France called the Western Front. Here, a new and horrific form of warfare developed.

The creation of the Western Front

In August 1914, it was commonly assumed that the **Great War** (as it soon became known) would be over by Christmas. Only a handful of far-sighted commanders, including the British war minister Lord Kitchener, predicted that it might last for years. The chief reason the war went on for so long was that it soon degenerated into a new and seemingly unwinnable form of combat: **trench warfare**.

For its first few months, the war was fought as a conventional 'war of movement', with mobile armies confronting each other in traditional battles. The Germans advanced far into France, almost reaching Paris, but were stopped in early September at the Battle of the Marne. Yet after the Germans had withdrawn slightly to a line north of the River Aisne, neither side could advance; instead, they both began moving northward in order to outflank one another. This developed into a 'race to the sea' that ended only when both armies had reached the English Channel in late October. As winter drew in, the Germans and the Allies faced each other along a 700-kilometre line, stretching right across France from the Channel to the border with Switzerland.

Accepting that they could launch no more offensives until the spring, the armies dug systems of fortified trenches that could house soldiers indefinitely and could be defended with machine guns against any attack. The result was a pair of opposed, immobile defensive systems, facing each other all along the line. This was the **Western Front**. Neither side realised that both armies would now be stuck in these trenches, with years of stalemate ahead.

The Eastern Front

Just as armies entrenched themselves on the Western Front, so the same process occurred in Eastern Europe, where German and Austro-Hungarian soldiers faced the Russians. Trench warfare became normal in both theatres of war.

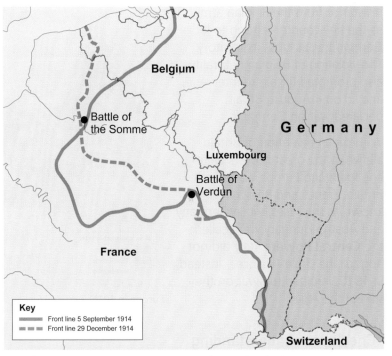

Map showing the Western Front, 1914, with 1916 battle sites

Trench warfare

Trench warfare created a situation in which any frontal attack on the enemy's positions, by either side, was almost inevitably doomed to failure.

When soldiers climbed out of their trenches and attempted to charge towards the enemy lines – known as going 'over the top' – they were easily slaughtered by machine-gun fire. Soldiers in a trench manning the gun emplacements could not easily be shot at themselves, but could mow down any approaching enemy. In the area of unoccupied land between the opposing sets of trenches, known as '**No Man's Land**', barbed wire was laid out in order to slow down any attack. The combination of machine guns and barbed wire made it almost impossible for any men to cross from their own trenches to the enemy's without being shot in the attempt.

The result was that the war became a static war, in which armies occupied the same positions, fighting from the same trenches, day in and day out, for years on end. Unable to break through the enemy positions, generals on both sides persisted in sending more men over the top, in increasingly massive and futile offensives. With territorial gain out of the question, the objective became simply to kill as many men as possible. This **war of attrition** focused on grinding down the enemy, making them use up their men and resources, until one side or the other was no longer able to fight.

Soldiers would take turns to sleep and keep watch in the trenches

Life in the trenches

For the men who lived and fought in these trenches, life could be gruelling. Built as temporary shelters, the trenches were shallow and muddy, offering little protection from the elements. Soldiers slept in 'foxholes' in the sides of their dug-outs. At any time, a trench might come under bombardment by the enemy's heavy **artillery**, and the Western Front quickly became a mass of craters left by shelling. Lice and rats were soldiers' constant companions, and some soldiers reported rats as large as cats, grown huge from feeding on rotting corpses. Soldiers were regularly rotated so that they would not be permanently at the front: they would normally spend around a week in the frontline trenches, before being rotated to reserve lines where they could wash, rest and recover.

In the cold and wet conditions, diseases spread through the trenches uncontrollably. One of the worst conditions was known as trench foot. Soldiers were forbidden to ever take off their boots, in case of a sudden attack. This meant that in freezing and rain-soaked trenches, a man's feet could lose blood supply and literally rot in his boots.

Poison gas

Chlorine, phosgene and mustard gas were used by both sides in the First World War. A gas attack could cause permanent damage, including blindness, or kill by choking or suffocation.

Check your understanding

1. What common expectations did people hold about the First World War when it began?
2. Why did both the Allies and the Germans dig trench systems along the Western Front in late 1914?
3. Why was it almost impossible for soldiers to directly attack entrenched positions?
4. How did generals on both sides respond to the stalemate on the Western Front?
5. What made life so unpleasant for soldiers stationed in the trenches?

The Battle of the Somme

In 1916, the British attempted to break the stalemate on the Western Front with a massive new offensive. The result was one of the most terrible battles British soldiers had ever fought.

In February of 1916, the Germans had begun an intense assault on the French areas of the front around **Verdun**. The purpose of this offensive, in the words of the German commander Erich von Falkenhayn, was "to bleed the French white". As the Battle of Verdun raged on for month after month, the British general Sir Douglas Haig planned to launch a new offensive against the German trenches near the River **Somme**. His aim was to take the pressure off the French by forcing the Germans to shift their troops to the Somme. Haig also hoped that if the assault was big and forceful enough, he might finally break through the German lines.

General Sir Douglas Haig

Haig's plan

Haig believed he had devised a way to break the entrenched stalemate. Before the battle, he launched a week-long artillery bombardment in which 1.7 million shells were fired. This was designed to break up the barbed wire and smash the German trench systems. With few German defences left, attacking British troops would then be able to walk – rather than run – across No Man's Land. This meant they could carry heavy packs and trench repair equipment, ready to take over and rebuild the German trenches. The army would move forward easily and huge swathes of land would be retaken.

What Haig did not understand was that the Germans, stationed on French territory and planning neither to retreat nor to advance in the foreseeable future, had built much deeper and better-fortified trench systems than the Allies. Reinforced concrete bunkers, nine metres deep, were hardly affected by the shelling. The bombardment therefore did little real damage. It did not help that many of the British shells were of poor quality, and up to 30 per cent of them failed to explode. As for the barbed wire, which was stretched along the front in a band more

British artillery ('howitzers') firing shells on the German line during the Battle of the Somme, 1916

than 30 metres wide, it was simply tossed up into the air by the explosions and then fell down again in roughly the same places.

The battle

In the early morning of 1 July 1916, two enormous **mines** (explosives placed beneath the enemy trenches by tunnellers known as sappers) were detonated. Then, at 7.30 am, 750 000 British soldiers went over the top. However, the expectation of an easy advance turned out to be disastrously wrong. The Germans, safe in their reinforced bunkers, were able to machine-gun the advancing British just as they always had done. To make matters worse, the advancing British soldiers were funnelled through the small number of narrow gaps in the barbed wire littering No Man's Land, making them obvious targets for German machine gunners. Over 19 000 were killed on the first day of the Somme, and around 38 000 were wounded. It was the single deadliest day in British military history.

Allied troops advancing through barbed wire during the Battle of the Somme

Haig pressed on with the offensive for months, despite criticism that he was simply throwing men to their deaths. As the battle went on he did make certain innovations, including using tanks (a new invention) in combat for the first time. Unfortunately, the Western Front was a bad environment for tanks: they quickly sank and got stuck in the thick mud, making them mostly useless. In the end, despite months of slaughter, there was no great breakthrough. When the offensive was called off on 18 November, a strip of land 25 km long and 6 km wide had been taken. For this tiny sliver of territory, 420 000 British and 200 000 French had been wounded or killed. General Sir Douglas Haig would come to be remembered by many as the 'Butcher of the Somme'.

As the year 1917 began, soldiers on all sides were deeply **disillusioned** with the war. For many people, the experience of trench warfare made the traditional values of chivalry, honour and patriotism seem empty and meaningless. Fighting and dying 'for king and country' had once been almost universally accepted as the right thing for a man to do. After the Great War, these ideals would be questioned and criticised much more widely than they ever had before.

Fact

Over 2.5 million soldiers from Britain's global empire fought for Britain in the First World War, including 1.3 million from India alone. At the Battle of the Somme, there were soldiers not only from Britain, but also from Australia, New Zealand, India, the West Indies, and various African colonies.

Check your understanding

1. Why did the British begin an offensive on the Somme in 1916?

2. How did General Sir Douglas Haig believe he could break the stalemate on the Western Front with this offensive?

3. Why did Haig's plan fail?

4. What was achieved in the Battle of the Somme, and at what cost?

5. How were values and attitudes towards the war beginning to change by the end of 1916?

Unit 1: The First World War
The wider war

The slaughter on the Western Front and Eastern Front was not the only fighting to take place during the First World War. Outside of Europe, other theatres of war were just as fiercely contested.

In late 1914, the **Ottoman Empire** joined the war on the side of the Central Powers. The Ottoman Empire was an old and mighty Turkish power that ruled not only **Asia Minor** (modern Turkey) but most of the Middle East as well. The British immediately began making plans to strike at the Ottomans in any way they could.

Gallipoli

The Ottoman capital, Constantinople (present-day Istanbul), could be reached only by sailing through the narrow straits of the **Dardanelles**. Winston Churchill, who was the First Lord of the Admiralty (head of the Royal Navy), believed that if the Dardanelles could be captured, this would open the way for a direct attack on Constantinople. The Ottoman Empire could then be knocked out of the war. Churchill planned to land an army on the Dardanelles at a place called Gallipoli. He planned that Allied troops would overwhelm the Turkish defences and make it possible for British warships to capture the straits.

An army was assembled consisting not only of British and French troops, but also a large contingent of **ANZACs** (Australian and New Zealand Army Corps). On 25 April 1915, the assault began on the coastline near Gallipoli. It was a disaster from the start: the soldiers found themselves facing steep cliffs and having to fight uphill towards heavily defended Turkish trenches. The Turks were commanded by a brilliant young colonel named Mustafa Kemal, whose successful defence of the Dardanelles made him an Ottoman war hero.

British troops attempt to land under Turkish machine-gun fire at Seduul Bahr in Galipoli, 25 April 1915

The campaign carried on for eight months, but eventually all Allied troops had to be evacuated after making almost no progress. The Gallipoli campaign cost 220 000 killed and wounded and achieved nothing. Churchill's reputation was ruined – though this did not turn out to be the end of his career.

Gertrude Bell

In 1915, the archaeologist and writer Gertrude Bell, a specialist on the Middle East, became the first woman ever employed by British military intelligence. She had spent her career travelling alone in the region and had many valuable contacts among the Arabs, so she was ideally placed to advise the British military on strategy and negotiations.

The Arab Revolt

The Arab people of the Middle East had been under Ottoman rule for centuries. Now that the empire was under attack, many of them planned to make a push for independence. The British hoped that they could bring down the Ottoman Empire from within by supporting these Arab tribes.

From their colony in Egypt, the British made contact with Hussein bin Ali, the Sharif (local ruler) of Mecca. After complex negotiations, they recognised him as the independent ruler of the Hejaz (western Arabia). The British promised that if the Ottomans could be defeated, they would support the creation of an independent Arab kingdom under Sharif Hussein. In June 1916, armed and supported by Britain, Hussein began a military uprising against the Ottomans. This was the **Arab Revolt**.

In 1917, Arab armies captured Aqaba at the northern end of the Red Sea and began moving northward into Syria. Simultaneously, a British army under General Edmund Allenby advanced from Egypt into Palestine, capturing Jerusalem in December. By October 1918, the combined Arab and British armies had captured Damascus and Aleppo, the two key cities of Syria, and the Turkish armies were defeated.

On 30 October 1918, the Ottoman Empire surrendered. This was the end of the empire, as it was divided after the war into several new nations and new European colonies. The Turks kept control only of Asia Minor, which in 1923 became the nation of Turkey. It was Mustafa Kemal, the hero of Gallipoli, who founded the new country and became its first president. He later became known as Atatürk, which means 'Father of the Turks'.

Camel corps in the desert at Beersheba, during the Sinai and Palestine Campaign of 1915–18

Lawrence of Arabia

T. E. Lawrence was a British army officer (and a student of Gertrude Bell) who was sent to negotiate with the Arabs in 1916. He was deeply impressed by the Arabs and formed a close friendship with Hussein's son Faisal. Lawrence felt that the Arab way of life was superior to the European, and he took to wearing Arab clothes and living by Arab customs. He played a key part in the Arab Revolt and frequently commanded Arab troops in battle.

After the war, Lawrence became a popular hero in Britain and was known as 'Lawrence of Arabia'. However, he had grown angry with the British, as he blamed them for breaking their promises to the Arabs when the war was over (see Unit 9, Chapter 2). He resisted becoming a celebrity, and he died in a motorcycle crash in 1935.

T. E. Lawrence in Arabian dress, circa 1917

Check your understanding

1. Why would it have been valuable for the Allies to gain control of the Dardanelles?

2. What were the outcomes of the Gallipoli campaign?

3. Why did Britain form an alliance with Arab forces under Sharif Hussein in 1916?

4. What was the outcome of the Arab Revolt?

5. Why did T. E. Lawrence become a popular war hero in Britain after the war?

Unit 1: The First World War
Allied victory

After years of fighting, many soldiers and civilians had lost faith in the war, and there was deep disillusionment on all sides. However, the direction of the war completely changed in 1917.

By 1917, Germany was suffering and struggling to continue fighting – but not because of events on the battlefield. Since the beginning of the conflict, the British had been using their navy to **blockade** Germany. This meant stopping and preventing ships carrying supplies from reaching German ports, thus starving German industry of the raw materials it needed. The blockade worked: German trade fell from $5.9 billion to $0.8 billion between 1914 and 1917, and German civilians were soon experiencing severe shortages of food and fuel.

Painting of *RMS Lusitania* torpedoed by a German submarine

In response to the blockade, German **U-boats** (submarines) launched attacks on Allied shipping. In 1915, the Germans declared 'unrestricted submarine warfare', which meant their U-boats could attack without warning and target civilian as well as military vessels – ignoring the conventional rules of naval combat. It was this U-boat campaign that would eventually tip the scales of the war decisively by bringing in a new and strong combatant on the Allied side.

America in, Russia out

On 7 May 1915, a German U-boat torpedoed and sank the British passenger liner ***RMS Lusitania***. Among the 1198 people killed, 128 were Americans, and the attack provoked outrage in the United States. Over the following years, American ships suspected of carrying supplies to Britain and France were also targeted. Eventually, in response to increasing popular pressure, President Woodrow Wilson brought the USA into the war on the side of the Allies, on 6 April 1917. This was a major departure from the traditional US policy of **isolationism**: keeping out of the affairs of Europe.

The Americans took many months to arrive in Europe in significant numbers, but the money they provided for supplies and armaments rejuvenated the Allied war effort. Within the same year, however, a second political change brought an unexpected change of fortunes for the Germans. Following the Bolshevik Revolution in October (see Unit 2, Chapter 2), Russia made peace with Germany and withdrew from the war. The Eastern Front was closed down, and large numbers of German troops could now be transferred to the west.

American soldiers in a front line trench during the Meuse-Argonne Offensive

The final offensives

With German civilians starving, and with almost 300 000 American troops already in France, Germany needed a quick victory. Three years of attrition and blockade had left their troops exhausted, underequipped and underfed, while newer recruits were badly trained and ill-disciplined. These men would be no match for the Americans. The renowned general Erich von Ludendorff, by now the leading figure in the German army, saw this clearly. Ludendorff therefore gambled on a final, massive offensive in the spring of 1918, designed to smash through France and win the war before the Americans could make too great a difference.

The Ludendorff Offensive, as it became known, was remarkably successful at first. This was because Ludendorff had devised new battlefield tactics that at last managed to break the stalemate on the Western Front. He used small bands of lightly equipped, fast-moving 'storm troops' to punch through the Allied line at weak points all along the front, rather than sending a massive wave of troops to attack a single point. This worked, and German soldiers poured through the gaps, managing to advance 64 kilometres. The Great War was briefly a war of movement again. However, the offensive cost 400 000 men, and by this time, Germany was completely out of reserves. The advance outran their supply lines, and the Allies inevitably began to push back.

From 8 August, the Allies launched their own massive counterattack all along the Western Front. Known as the **Hundred Days Offensive**, this campaign relied on large numbers of new and well-trained troops, ample supplies and first-rate equipment – all thanks to American contributions. By October, the Germans were in full retreat, abandoning their trenches and pulling back out of France. Recognising defeat, Kaiser Wilhelm II abdicated on 9 November. Two days later, on 11 November 1918, the two sides signed an **armistice**, and the fighting at last came to an end.

Legacy

The First World War was the most brutal and destructive conflict the world had ever seen. It took the lives of between 9 and 11 million soldiers, and around 8 million civilians. It ended the confidence of 19th-century Europe in progress and improvement, giving rise to an age of uncertainty, violence and political upheaval across the continent. Finally, by pushing Russia into revolution and leaving Germany broken and humiliated, the war planted the seeds for an even greater and more terrible conflict that would engulf the world in just over 30 years.

The end of Austria-Hungary

Under economic blockade along with the Germans, the people of the Austro-Hungarian empire had been starving for years. When it became clear that the Allies were going to win the war, they began pressing for independence. In the final few months of 1918, the empire's Balkan Slavic population (Serbs, Croats and Slovenes) joined with independent Serbia to form the new state of Yugoslavia, while Poles, Hungarians and Czechs all declared their own states. With dramatic speed, the Austro-Hungarian empire fell apart.

Check your understanding

1. What were the effects of the British naval blockade of Germany?

2. Why did the United States enter the war against Germany?

3. What made the Ludendorff Offensive different from previous attacks on the Western Front?

4. Why did the Austro-Hungarian empire cease to exist at the end of 1918?

5. When and how did the First World War come to an end?

Unit 1: The First World War
Knowledge organiser

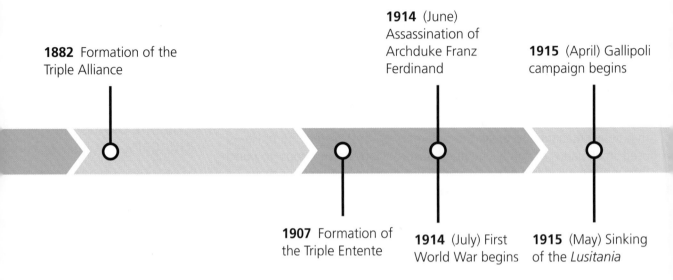

1882 Formation of the Triple Alliance

1914 (June) Assassination of Archduke Franz Ferdinand

1915 (April) Gallipoli campaign begins

1907 Formation of the Triple Entente

1914 (July) First World War begins

1915 (May) Sinking of the *Lusitania*

Key vocabulary

ANZACs The Australian and New Zealand Army Corps; troops from these countries who fought for Britain in the First World War

Arab Revolt Rebellion against Ottoman rule by the Arabs during the First World War, supported by Britain

Armistice Agreement to stop fighting or to end a war

Artillery Heavy, wheeled guns that fire large explosive shells

Asia Minor Region now occupied by Turkey, previously the heartland of the Ottoman Empire

Austria-Hungary Central European empire that disintegrated after the First World War

Balance of power Situation in which peace is preserved because opposing nations have roughly equal power

Black Hand Serbian nationalist terrorist organisation

Blockade Use of warships or other military force to stop a nation from trading

Central Powers Wartime name for Germany, Austria-Hungary and their allies

Dardanelles Narrow straits that separate the Mediterranean Sea from Istanbul (Constantinople) and the Black Sea

Disillusionment Loss of beliefs or ideals about something after discovering that it does not match what was expected or imagined

Great War Alternative name for the First World War, used by those at the time

Hundred Days Offensive Allied offensive that ended the First World War in 1918

Isolationism National policy of avoiding becoming involved in other nations' problems or conflicts

Lusitania British passenger ship (carrying some American passengers) sunk by a German U-boat in 1915 with the loss of 1198 lives

Mines Explosives placed in the ground beneath enemy fortifications or trenches

No Man's Land Term for the area between two opposed trench systems

Ottoman Empire Turkish empire that ruled the Middle East and parts of Europe and Africa from the 14th century to 1918

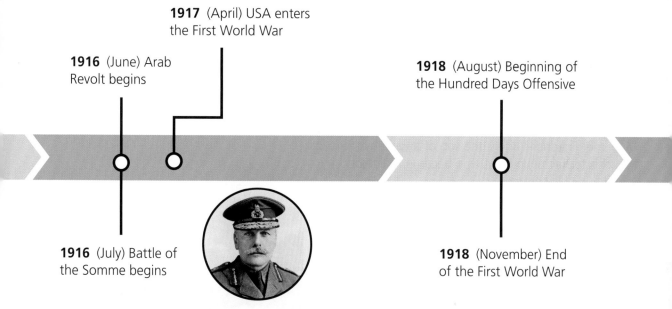

1917 (April) USA enters the First World War

1916 (June) Arab Revolt begins

1918 (August) Beginning of the Hundred Days Offensive

1916 (July) Battle of the Somme begins

1918 (November) End of the First World War

Key vocabulary

Schlieffen Plan German plan to begin any war by attacking France with maximum force, and only later turn on Russia

Somme (Battle of the) Long and destructive battle fought in 1916 by the British on the Western Front

Trench warfare Warfare based on defensive trench systems, in which neither side can gain the advantage

Triple Alliance Defensive alliance formed in 1882 between Germany, Italy and Austria-Hungary

Triple Entente Defensive alliance formed in 1907 between Britain, France and Russia

U-boat German term for a submarine

Verdun (Battle of) German assault on the French in 1916

War of attrition Warfare focused on forcing the enemy to use up their men and resources until they can no longer fight

Western Front Area of battle during the First World War in Belgium and France, consisting of Allied and German trench systems facing each other

Key people

Hussein bin Ali Sharif of Mecca, leader of the Arab Revolt

Mustafa Kemal Atatürk Known as 'Father of the Turks', Ottoman commander who led the defence at Gallipoli and later became the founder of post-Ottoman Turkey

Gertrude Bell British archaeologist who became a key military intelligence advisor on the Middle East

Archduke Franz Ferdinand Heir to the throne of Austria-Hungary, whose assassination sparked the First World War

Douglas Haig British general who launched the Battle of the Somme

T. E. Lawrence British officer who became a famous war hero as 'Lawrence of Arabia' for his role fighting alongside the Arabs

Gavrilo Princip Serbian assassin from the 'Black Hand' who shot Franz Ferdinand

Kaiser Wilhelm II Emperor of Germany before and during the First World War

Woodrow Wilson American president from 1913 to 1921 who brought the USA into the war

Unit 2: The USSR
Marx and Communism

In the 19th century, the economist and philosopher Karl Marx developed a new way of thinking about human societies that would go on to influence revolutionaries throughout the world.

Marx was born in Germany in 1818, the son of a Jewish lawyer. He studied law himself then became a journalist and moved to Paris. Here, Marx met Friedrich Engels, the son of a wealthy Manchester factory owner, who became his lifelong friend and collaborator.

At this time, Europe was being transformed by the Industrial Revolution that had begun in 18th-century England. Huge numbers of people had moved from the countryside into the cities to become workers in the new factories, and they often worked 12-hour days and lived in filthy and overcrowded slums. Marx and Engels were appalled by the misery of the workers and the inequality of industrial society. In 1844, Engels wrote a book called *The Condition of the Working Class in England* that condemned the working and living conditions in cities such as Manchester.

Textile workers in a Manchester factory in the mid-19th century

Capitalism and Socialism

Marx came to feel that the root of the problem was **capitalism**. Capitalism is a system of social organisation that has been accepted in most of Western Europe since before the Industrial Revolution, and remains standard to this day. Under capitalism, all people are free to buy and sell as they choose, work in whatever jobs they can get, and try to make as much money as they can. Prices and wages are determined not by laws or regulations, but by competition – as employers who pay too low wages will lose their workers, and merchants who charge too high prices will not sell very much. In theory, capitalism maximises the creation of wealth, and this eventually raises living standards for everyone.

Marx believed that, in practice, capitalism leads to widening inequality and the exploitation of workers. He argued that capitalists – meaning factory owners and businessmen – collect the profits while workers are denied a fair share in the wealth that their labour creates. Marx argued that advanced capitalism would inevitably lead to a revolution by the workers.

These views were set out in a short book called the **Communist Manifesto**, which was published by Marx and Engels in 1848 – right as a wave of revolutions was sweeping Europe. Marx later moved to London and spent the rest of his life working on a much longer book, **Das Kapital**, which explained his economic theories in great detail. The last volumes of this book were not published until after Marx's death in 1883.

Karl Marx (1818–83)

Inspired by Marx, Socialist movements appeared throughout Europe. **Socialism** is an alternative form of economic organisation to capitalism. There are many varieties of Socialism, but all of them aim to give workers greater control over production, and distribute wealth more widely through society. The most radical form of Socialism is **Communism**, which aims to create near-total equality by abolishing private property and sharing all work and all goods among everybody.

Moderate Socialists believe in working within established society to improve conditions for workers. The British Labour Party was founded on this basis in the year 1900. More radical Marxists believe that the ruling classes would never allow serious, fundamental change within the capitalist system, so the whole structure of society needs to be overthrown before a new and better society can be built. Marxist revolutionaries were feared by established governments, who saw them as a serious threat to peace, democracy and social order.

Class theory

Marxist theory divides society into the aristocracy (upper class), the **bourgeoisie** (middle class), and the **proletariat** (working class). It states that societies evolve by going through a series of revolutions in which different classes take power. First, the bourgeoisie takes power from the aristocracy and creates a capitalist society. Then, the proletariat takes power and creates a Communist society run by the workers.

Marxism in Russia

Russia in the early 20th century was the last place that anyone expected a Communist revolution to occur. Marxist theory held that working-class revolution would take place in industrial countries when capitalism became intolerable for ordinary people. This meant that Marxists expected revolution in the most advanced industrial nations: Britain and Germany. However, Russia was not an advanced industrial nation.

Russian peasant workers photographed in 1913

Under its emperors, the **Tsars**, Russia was a mostly unmodernised country in which a small number of nobles dominated a large population of peasants. Industry and commerce lagged behind the other powers of Europe, and even by 1896, only 15 per cent of Russians lived in towns. Nicholas II, Russia's Tsar since 1894, was a weak and tyrannical ruler. He resisted all efforts to introduce democracy in Russia or to grant basic freedoms to his people.

Though there was a Marxist revolutionary movement in Russia, most of them accepted that the revolution was a long way off. As they saw it, Russia had not yet even had its bourgeois (middle-class) revolution – so it could not be ready for a workers' revolution.

Check your understanding

1. Why were Karl Marx and Friedrich Engels angered by living conditions for working people in their time?
2. What are the basic principles of capitalism?
3. What did Marx believe about capitalism?
4. What were the aims of the Socialist movements inspired by Marx's writings?
5. Why was Russia not a place where Marxists expected a workers' revolution to occur?

Unit 2: The USSR
The Russian Revolution

During the First World War (1914–18), life in Russia grew steadily worse. The war took the lives of an estimated 1.8 million Russian men on the Eastern Front, and created chronic shortages of food and fuel.

There was a string of military failures, beginning with a disastrous defeat at Tannenberg in East Prussia (modern-day Poland) at the very start of the war. In August 1915, Nicholas II took personal command of the army in order to try to turn things around. However, this left the Russian government in the hands of the Tsarina (empress), Alexandra, who was even less competent than her husband – and who was under the sway of the mysterious Rasputin (see box). Subsequently, the Russian people grew more and more angry with the Tsarist regime.

Rasputin

In Nicholas II's Russia, unusual power was held by a religious mystic named Grigory Rasputin. He had been brought to the court to treat the Tsar's son, Alexei, who suffered from haemophilia. Some saw Rasputin as a prophet with magical powers, while others thought he was a fraud. In 1916, Rasputin was murdered by Russian nobles who thought he had too much influence over Alexandra.

The February Revolution

In February 1917, women workers in Petrograd (the Russian capital, now called St. Petersburg) marked International Women's Day with a strike to demand bread. Their demonstration sparked a series of strikes and demonstrations that brought 200 000 protesters onto the streets. The uprising quickly spread to peasant revolts in the countryside, protests in other major cities, and soldiers' and sailors' mutinies. The Tsarist system collapsed almost overnight, and the Tsar and his family were taken prisoner by the revolutionaries.

There was immediate disagreement over what should replace the Tsarist system. A collection of officials from the Tsar's government formed a **Provisional Government** (meaning temporary government) to run the country until something new could be established. Real control, however, lay elsewhere. During the February Revolution, striking workers and soldiers across the country had formed independent governing councils to make collective decisions and oversee reforms. These councils were called '**Soviets**'. It was the Soviets, and above all the Petrograd Soviet, that exercised practical control over the country and could influence or direct the workers and soldiers.

The Russian people were calling for a democratic parliament, redistribution of land, stable food supplies and, above all, an end to Russia's involvement

Cartoon of 1917 showing Rasputin (centre) with the Tsar (bottom right) and Tsarina (centre left), and Russia's military leaders

in the First World War. As the year dragged on, the Provisional Government and its leader Alexander Kerensky proved unable or unwilling to introduce any of these changes. Popular frustration grew, and in July there were mass demonstrations against the Provisional Government. "All power to the Soviets!" became the rallying cry of the revolution. There were mass desertions from the front, as soldiers, unwilling to continue fighting a war they viewed as meaningless, simply left the trenches and walked away. Angry and desperate for change, many Russian workers threw their support behind the one political party that seemed willing to take direct action: the **Bolsheviks**.

The Bolsheviks

The Bolsheviks were a radical Marxist party led by a passionate and determined man named Vladimir Lenin. Lenin had an unusual interpretation of Marxism: he believed that an elite revolutionary group called a **vanguard** could seize power on behalf of the workers, even if the workers themselves were not yet 'ready' for Communism. The Bolsheviks were Lenin's vanguard party. Lenin had set out these ideas in 1902 in a pamphlet entitled 'What is to be Done?' For most of the years since, he had lived in exile in various parts of Europe. In April 1917, Lenin returned to Russia, declaring that the time for Communist revolution had arrived.

Vladimir Lenin
(1870–1924)

Leon Trotksy
(1879–1940)

Lenin was soon joined by another prominent Russian radical who had also been in exile: Leon Trotsky. The two men had a history of disagreements, as Trotsky had long advocated a more democratic approach to Socialism. However, in 1917 Trotsky decided that the Bolsheviks were Russia's best hope, and he accepted Lenin's leadership. He soon became chairman of the Petrograd Soviet, giving the Bolsheviks significantly greater influence in politics. Trotsky was an inspiring public speaker and a talented writer, but he was arrogant and often quarrelled with his allies, so he made many enemies within the Party.

The October Revolution

Alarmed by growing support for the Bolsheviks, on 24 October Kerensky attempted to arrest the leading revolutionaries in Petrograd. In response, the Bolsheviks launched an armed takeover of the government the very same day, with Trotsky commanding the Bolshevik troops. On 25 October the Bolsheviks stormed the **Winter Palace**, a former imperial residence that was the headquarters of the Provisional Government. Leading members of the Provisional Government were captured – though Kerensky escaped, later settling in the USA. By the morning of 26 October, the Bolsheviks had secured power in Petrograd. Russia's second revolution of 1917 had produced the first Communist government in the history of the world.

Check your understanding

1. Why did the Tsarist government collapse in February 1917?

2. What were the Soviets?

3. Why did many Russian people soon grow dissatisfied with the Provisional Government?

4. What were Vladimir Lenin's beliefs about revolution?

5. Why did the Bolsheviks overthow the Provisional Government in October 1917?

Unit 2: The USSR
From Lenin to Stalin

Once in power, the Bolsheviks established a '**dictatorship of the proletariat**'. In theory this meant a government run by the workers, but in practice their regime kept all power in Bolshevik hands.

One of Lenin's first acts in power was to end Russian participation in the First World War, in March 1918. In the countryside, private ownership of land was abolished, and all estates were shared out among the peasants while landlords received no compensation. All titles, class distinctions, and even ranks in the army were abolished, and people instead began to call each other '**comrade**'.

In November 1917, elections were held for the **Constituent Assembly**, Russia's first-ever democratic parliament. However, the Bolsheviks won less than a quarter of the vote. By far the biggest share went to a different Marxist party called the Socialist Revolutionaries, who had widespread support among the Russian peasants. Lenin claimed that this result was an expression of 'bourgeois' attitudes and did not represent the Russian people's true political will. He therefore shut down the Constituent Assembly after just one day.

From this point on, the Bolsheviks began banning other political parties, closing newspapers that criticised them, and imprisoning their political opponents. Lenin became effectively a dictator.

A White Russian poster of 1920 showing a white knight attacking a red Bolshevik dragon

The Russian Civil War

From 1918 to 1922, Russia was engulfed by civil war, as anti-Bolshevik forces called the **Whites** attempted to reverse the October Revolution. Britain, France, the United States and multiple other nations all sent troops to fight alongside the Whites. The Western governments were frightened of Communist revolution, and so they sought to suppress the Bolsheviks before their example could spread to other nations. The Whites were mostly led by former Tsarist officers, and they massacred peasants and performed mass public torture in order to establish their dominance. However, the Bolsheviks were just as ruthless, killing tens of thousands of rebel soldiers and peasants who refused to obey their directives.

As many as 10 million Russians died in the Russian Civil War, around four times the Russian death toll in the First World War. During the conflict, the Bolsheviks instituted conscription, confiscated food supplies to feed their new **Red Army**, and imprisoned and murdered political opponents in the 'Red Terror' (red is traditionally the colour of Communism). In the end, the Red Army won the war because it was disciplined, united and had

The Russian Revolution, civil war and drought led to famine in Russia

strong leadership in Leon Trotsky. The peasants generally supported the Bolsheviks because they feared a return of their landlords if the Whites were victorious. All the same, the war effort caused many of them to lose faith in their new leaders.

Having defeated the Whites, the Bolsheviks created a new country called the Union of Soviet Socialist Republics (USSR), or **Soviet Union**. In the USSR, all decisions were taken by the leadership of the Bolshevik party, renamed the Communist Party, which was headed by a council called the **Politburo**. The Communists controlled all parts of the new Soviet government.

The new leader

From 1922 onwards, Lenin suffered a series of strokes that left him increasingly incapable of taking an active part in government. A power struggle began among the leading Communist Party officials. Lenin's preferred successor seemed to be Trotsky, but Trotsky faced a powerful rival. This was Josef Stalin (a name he had chosen himself, meaning 'Man of Steel'). Stalin had been a high-ranking Bolshevik for over 10 years, and he had gradually secured a number of important administrative roles in the Party, including the powerful postition of General Secretary. Even so, he was often overlooked and under-estimated because he seemed quiet and unintellectual, lacking the strong personality of Lenin or Trotsky. In fact, Stalin was ambitious, ruthless, very intelligent, and obsessed with gaining total power over the USSR.

Stalin and Trotsky had very different visions of their country's future. Trotsky believed in 'permanent revolution', meaning that the Soviet leadership should direct an international and ongoing revolutionary movement to spread Communism around the world. Stalin believed in 'Socialism in one country', meaning that the Soviets should focus on defending Communism in their own territory rather than spreading it elsewhere.

After Lenin died in January 1924, Stalin moved quickly to oppose the rise of Trotsky. With the help of his allies Grigory Zinoviev and Lev Kamenev, Stalin had Trotsky demoted from his position as war **commissar** (war minister) in January 1925. He then turned on Zinoviev and Kamenev, and had them demoted too. Trotsky was expelled from the Communist Party in 1927, and exiled from the USSR in 1929. By that year, Stalin had secured total political control within the Communist Party. He was now the unchallenged dictator of the USSR.

Fact

On 17 July 1918, Nicholas II, his wife, and their five children were executed by firing squad. The Bolsheviks feared that if the imperial family were recaptured by White forces, they would give the Whites a powerful way to rally opposition to the new regime.

Josef Stalin (1878–1953)

Check your understanding

1. How did Lenin respond to the results of the Constituent Assembly elections?

2. Why did Western governments aid the Whites in the Russian Civil War?

3. What methods did the Bolsheviks employ in order to win the Russian Civil War?

4. How did Trotsky and Stalin disagree about the future of the USSR?

5. How had Stalin become dictator of the USSR by 1929?

Unit 2: The USSR
Stalin's tyranny

Under Stalin's rule, the USSR did not create a better society for most Soviet workers. Instead it evolved into a ruthless **totalitarian** empire.

A totalitarian political system is one in which individuals have no freedom and everything is directed by the state. Stalin ruled Russia with much greater severity than the Tsars had done. He was sometimes said by his enemies to be like a 'Red Tsar'.

Agriculture and industry

Stalin's first major reform was to launch the process of **collectivisation** in the countryside. This meant that peasants were forced to give up their private farms and become part of communally managed farms called 'collectives'. Stalin claimed that ordinary peasants were being exploited by richer peasants called **kulaks**, and collectivisation was the only way to 'liberate' them. In fact this was a myth – there was almost no significant conflict between different classes of peasants. Nonetheless, the *kulaks* were targeted and their households were stripped of everything they owned. Often, they anticipated this by slaughtering their own animals and destroying their own equipment, rather than handing them over to the state. Soviet policy was encouraging the active destruction of useful resources.

By 1930, some 1–3 million *kulaks* had been arrested, and 30 000 had been shot. A few years later, Stalin's attempts to reorganise rural life led to a disastrous famine. Collectivisation and bad harvests combined to create massive food shortages in many areas of the Soviet Union, especially in Ukraine and Kazakhstan in 1932–3, with at least 5 million people estimated to have starved to death. The crisis was made worse by Soviet policy: peasants were shot for eating their own grain rather than handing it over to Communist authorities, and discussion of the crisis was banned. However, Stalin did not change course: collectivisation went on, and by the end of 1937, 93 per cent of peasants had been collectivised.

Stalin knew that the USSR lagged behind the West in economic development, and he wanted to modernise Soviet industry. He therefore launched a series of **Five-Year Plans**: ambitious programs of industrialisation, building factories and driving up production at breakneck speed. In effect, Stalin was attempting an Industrial Revolution on a dramatically compressed timescale: what Britain had achieved over a century of industrial development, Stalin wanted to do in a handful of years.

> ### Fact
> A *kulak* was defined in 1925 as any peasant who owned at least three cows.

> ### Fact
> The Ukrainian famine is sometimes called the **Holodomor**, a Ukrainian name meaning 'murder by starvation'.

Large crowds of people wait for bread during the Russian 'Great Famine' of the 1930s

There were seven Five-Year Plans from 1929 to 1964, though some ended early because the Party declared they had succeeded ahead of schedule. Under these plans, production targets were set based on ideology rather than on what was actually possible, and factory managers were required to meet these targets in any way they could. Workers often worked 12-hour shifts or longer. When targets were not met, it was always said to be because workers or managers had cheated or hoarded resources, never because the targets had been unrealistic in the first place.

Paranoia and terror

Stalin was deeply **paranoid**, and constantly suspected even his closest allies of plotting against him. In the USSR, anybody suspected of opposing the regime, even of having disloyal thoughts, could be imprisoned, tortured or executed. The **NKVD**, Stalin's secret police, had spies and informants everywhere. The slightest remark even hinting at dissatisfaction with Communism could lead to swift arrest. This sometimes led to people **denouncing** others simply to get rid of those they disliked. In this way, Soviet rule spread mistrust throughout society.

Stalin's suspicion of 'opponents' escalated to extremes in 1936–8, a period known as 'the Great Terror'. The NKVD, under its new commissar Nikolai Yezhov, arrested high-ranking figures from the upper reaches of the Party and put them on trial in public **show trials**. These were staged performances in which, after extensive torture behind the scenes, people were forced to confess to imaginary crimes before being shot. An estimated 93 out of 139 members of the Party's Central Committee were arrested, as Stalin **purged** anyone and everyone who might threaten his control. In total, 7–8 million people were arrested during the Great Terror, and up to 1.5 million were shot. In addition, millions of people were sent to the **gulags** – the USSR's vast network of prison camps in Siberia. Death rates from forced labour in these camps were astronomically high.

This 1931 Soviet poster – "2 + 2 = 5. Arithmetic of the industrial and financial plan with the enthusiasm of the workers" – was produced after Stalin revealed the first Five-Year Plan would be completed nearly a year ahead of schedule

Fact

In 1940, Yezhov himself was shot on Stalin's orders. Even those who carried out his most paranoid commands were not safe from Stalin's suspicion.

Trotsky in exile

As Stalin's rule grew increasingly cruel, the exiled Trotsky became a figurehead for all who imagined an alternative, better form of Communism. Eventually, Stalin decided that it was too dangerous to let him live, and sent assassins to find and kill him. In 1940, a Spanish-born NKVD agent tracked Trotsky down in Mexico and murdered him with an ice pick.

Check your understanding

1. What was the policy of collectivisation?
2. How did collectivisation lead to famine in the Ukraine in 1932–3?
3. Why did the Five-Year Plans create such awful working conditions for Soviet workers?
4. How did the NKVD police the Soviet Union?
5. How did Stalin's paranoia grow more extreme during the late 1930s?

Life in the USSR

In the USSR, membership of the Communist Party **bureaucracy** (administrative system) was the only way to get a good career or a good home.

Communist ideology

Government jobs, university places and managerial roles in industry did not go to those who were most talented. Instead, they went to those who said the right things and acted like they were good Communists. Those who did not conform to official ideology had no chance of a better life. The Soviet leaders were determined not just to change society, but to engineer an entirely new type of human being, who they called 'Soviet man' or 'Soviet woman'. These new human beings were expected to be selfless, disciplined and enthusiastic about Socialist ideology. In order to create Soviet man and woman, every aspect of life in the Soviet Union was carefully controlled.

The Soviet newspaper **_Pravda_** (the name means 'Truth') expressed the official opinions of the Party, while all other publications were heavily **censored**. Records, including photographs, were regularly altered in order to make it seem like whatever was the current policy had always been the policy, and the leadership had never made any mistakes. Objective truth became harder and harder to pin down, as all information was controlled by the Party.

The USSR was officially atheist, and so the Orthodox Church (the main form of Christianity in the USSR) was persecuted. Artists, writers and musicians were instructed to promote appropriate Soviet ideals in their work. Under Lenin, the USSR had encouraged artistic experimentation, and some early Soviet painting, sculpture and filmmaking is still regarded as very important in modern art. However, under Stalin, all art was forced to conform to 'Socialist realism', which meant strictly realistic depictions of the lives of workers.

Statues and posters of Stalin himself were put up all over the USSR. This was part of a **cult of personality** that depicted Stalin as an immensely wise, all-powerful figure who was guiding the Soviet people into a better future. To reinforce this message, cities were renamed: the city of Tsaritsyn on the Volga River became Stalingrad, while Petrograd became Leningrad.

Living standards for ordinary Soviet people fell. By the late 1930s, workers' consumption of meat and fish had fallen by 80 per cent. Possibly the only area in which quality of life significantly improved was

'Monument to Worker and Peasant Woman', created in 1937 by Soviet sculptor Vera Muhina. The figures hold a sickle and hammer, representing proletarian solidarity.

Fact

When a round of applause broke out for Stalin at a Communist Party conference in 1937, the audience quickly realised that none of them dared to be the first person to stop clapping. The applause went on for 11 minutes before one man, the manager of a paper factory, finally stopped clapping and sat down. Everyone else also stopped immediately – but later that night, the man who had been first to stop clapping was arrested and sent to prison for 10 years.

Soviet propaganda poster of the 1930s, presenting Stalin as having opened the doors of education to the people

education, as the Soviets opened many new schools and universities, made attendance compulsory and oversaw rising literacy.

Women's rights in the USSR

When the Bolsheviks seized power in 1917, efforts were made to bring about gender equality. Alexandra Kollontai became the world's first female member of a governing cabinet in history, and set up the Zhenotdel to promote women's rights. Divorce was made easier, abortion was legalised and women did not need a husband's permission to take a job. However, in 1930 Stalin closed down the Zhenotdel, claiming women's issues in the Soviet Union had been 'solved'. The radical policies the Zhenotdel had introduced were reversed, and women were pushed out of politics to focus on traditional roles as housewives and mothers.

Alexandra Kollontai

Soviet anti-Semitism

In the wider world, anti-Semites often identified the USSR as a Jewish creation – partly because some of the original Bolshevik leaders, including Trotsky, had been Jewish. However, in reality, Jews in the USSR faced widespread anti-Semitism and were often persecuted. Stalin called Jews "rootless cosmopolitans", meaning people who did not truly belong anywhere.

After Stalin

In 1953, Josef Stalin died. His successor, Nikita Khrushchev, began a campaign of '**Destalinisation**'. Censorship was relaxed, political prisoners were released, and the cult of personality around Stalin was criticised. The Communist Party still held total power, but Khrushchev wanted to make the Soviet Union a less extreme, less repressive place.

In general, he succeeded. Under Khrushchev and the leaders who came after him, the USSR was no longer a place where huge numbers of people were regularly arrested or killed. Instead, the people were allowed to live mostly in peace, so long as they never challenged the Party or openly disagreed with official views. Living standards also eventually rose, and life was tolerable for most people. However, the original aims and ideals of the Russian Revolution were well and truly dead. In the later USSR, not many people really believed in a better Communist future anymore.

Check your understanding

1. What was meant by 'Soviet man' and 'Soviet woman'?
2. How did the Communist Party attempt to control information?
3. How did women's rights in the USSR change under Stalin?
4. How did Nikita Khrushchev attempt to change the USSR after he came to power?
5. How did official Communist ideology influence ordinary life in the USSR?

Unit 2: The USSR
Knowledge organiser

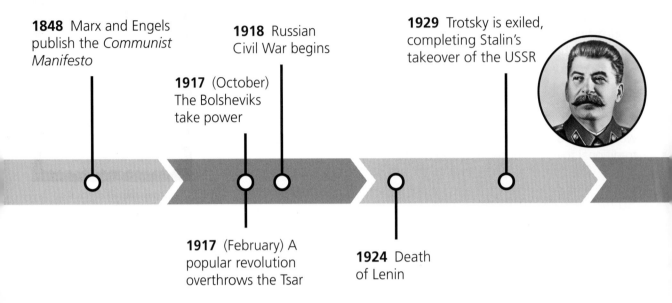

1848 Marx and Engels publish the *Communist Manifesto*

1918 Russian Civil War begins

1929 Trotsky is exiled, completing Stalin's takeover of the USSR

1917 (October) The Bolsheviks take power

1917 (February) A popular revolution overthrows the Tsar

1924 Death of Lenin

Key vocabulary

Bolsheviks Radical Russian Communist Party that founded the USSR

Bourgeoisie The middle classes, or those who make money through trade or industry

Bureaucracy An administrative system in a government

Capitalism Economic system based on the freedom to buy, sell and trade

Censor To prevent something from being said or published for political reasons

Collectivisation The process of combining privately owned farms into large 'collectives' farmed by groups of people under common ownership

Commissar Soviet term for an official or commander

Communism Economic system based on the equal distribution of land and resources

Communist Manifesto Short book by Karl Marx and Friedrich Engels that lays out the basic ideas of Communism

Comrade A colleague or fellow soldier; used as a general term of address in Marxist societies

Constituent Assembly Russian parliament elected in 1917 but dissolved by Lenin

Cult of personality The presentation of a national leader as a great figure who should be admired and loved

Das Kapital Book by Karl Marx explaining his theories in detail

Denounce To publicly condemn someone or something as bad or wrong

Destalinisation Process of reform in the Soviet Union launched by Khrushchev after Stalin's death

Dictatorship of the proletariat In Marxist theory, a government run by the workers following a revolution

Five-Year Plans Official programs of industrialisation in the Soviet Union

Gulag Prison camp in the Soviet Union

Holodomor The Ukrainian famine of 1932–3 that was caused by Stalin's policies

Kulak Soviet term for a richer peasant

NKVD The Soviet secret police

Paranoid Believing that there are enemies everywhere, or being constantly suspicious

Politburo Governing council of the Communist Party in the Soviet Union

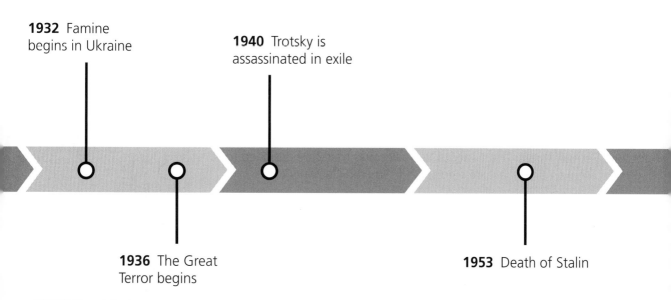

1932 Famine begins in Ukraine

1940 Trotsky is assassinated in exile

1936 The Great Terror begins

1953 Death of Stalin

Key vocabulary

Pravda Government-run newspaper in the Soviet Union

Proletariat The working classes, or those who depend on wage labour for their living

Provisional Government Temporary government formed to govern Russia after the February Revolution

Purge Removal of unwanted people from an organisation, usually in a violent way

Red Army The army of the USSR

Show trial Staged and scripted trial in which an opposition figure is forced to confess to imaginary crimes after torture behind the scenes

Socialism System of economic organisation that aims to distribute wealth widely through society

Soviet Originally a council of workers or soldiers formed in Russia after the February Revolution; later a term for citizens of the Soviet Union

Soviet Union Alternative name for the USSR

Totalitarianism Any political system that aims for total control over all aspects of people's lives

Tsar Emperor of Russia before the revolution

Vanguard A small group that leads the way, often in a military or revolutionary context

Whites Anti-Communist Russians

Winter Palace Tsarist residence that became the headquarters of the Provisional Government

Key people

Friedrich Engels Friend of Karl Marx who collaborated on much of his work

Alexander Kerensky Head of the Provisional Government

Alexandra Kollontai Leading Bolshevik who became the world's first female cabinet minister

Vladimir Lenin Leader of the Bolsheviks, who launched the 1917 October Revolution and created the USSR

Karl Marx German economist who developed the theory of Communism

Nicholas II The last Tsar of Russia, overthrown in the February Revolution

Josef Stalin Dictator of the USSR, who seized power after Lenin's death

Leon Trotsky Leading Bolshevik who became Stalin's main rival for leadership of the USSR

The Treaty of Versailles

The end of the First World War brought no true peace to Germany. Instead, the country entered a period of chaos that eventually gave birth to a whole new terror for Europe.

At the Paris Peace Conference of 1919, the victorious Allies produced the **Treaty of Versailles**, which dictated the terms of the peace to the defeated Germans. The British and French leaders, and especially French prime minister Georges Clemenceau, were determined to prevent any future German threat. The Treaty of Versailles was therefore designed to punish, weaken and humiliate Germany. It required Germany to:

- Give up 13 per cent of its territory, including losing land in the east to newly independent Poland, and the provinces of Alsace and Lorraine to France.
- Reduce its army to a mere 100 000 men, reduce its navy to six battleships, and give up its air force completely.
- Demilitarise the **Rhineland** (the region of Germany that borders France), meaning no German troops could ever be stationed there.
- Pay **reparations**, meaning payments by the defeated to the victors, of 132 billion gold marks (£6.6 billion).
- Formally accept responsibility for causing the war (the '**War Guilt Clause**').

This treaty provoked deep and enduring anger in Germany. Many on the Allied side correctly predicted that the perceived harshness of the treaty would fuel German resentment, seriously increasing the risk of future conflict. The French general Ferdinand Foch stated: "This is not a peace. It is an armistice for twenty years."

German poster of 1929 expressing resentment of the reparations Germany was made to pay by the terms of the Treaty of Versailles – a 'tribut' is a payment made by one country to another, here for '69 jahre' (years)

The Weimar Republic

The pre-war German empire was now replaced by a democracy known as the **Weimar Republic**, after the city of Weimar where its constitution was designed. However, the republic was never fully accepted by many German people, because they associated it with the Treaty of Versailles. Partly because Germany had never been physically invaded or occupied at the end of the war, many Germans wrongly believed they had not really lost the war on the battlefield. Unable to accept that Germany could have been defeated, they believed Germany had been betrayed by enemies within, and they blamed the defeat on minority groups such as socialists and Jews. This was the **'Stab in the Back' myth**. For those who believed in this myth, the Weimar government was not thought to be legitimate.

Hatred of the Weimar government was made worse by the economic turmoil that Germany suffered for years after the war. Regular reparations payments made it almost impossible for the German economy to recover, and in 1923 the economy collapsed. The currency went into

hyperinflation, which meant that prices rose staggeringly high and extraordinary fast. In January of 1923, a loaf of bread cost 250 marks, but by November it cost 200 billion marks. People's lifelong savings were suddenly worthless, and workers' wages were useless.

The rise of the Nazis

In this desperate time, anti-democratic extremists plotted against the Weimar state. One of these extremists was a young **anti-Semitic** nationalist named Adolf Hitler. In 1921, Hitler became the leader of a small far-right group called the National Socialist German Workers' Party (NSDAP), popularly dubbed the Nazis. Hitler was a talented speaker with a clear vision for a new Germany, and he attracted crowds of supporters with his long, intensely emotional speeches. He gathered a small but passionately loyal following, dedicated to the violent overthrow of the Weimar Republic and the creation of a new German empire that would be racially 'pure' and militarily expansionist.

Hitler was inspired by the **Fascist** movement that had recently emerged in Italy, led by Benito Mussolini. After Mussolini seized power in 1922 and turned Italy into the world's first Fascist state, Hitler attempted to follow in his footsteps. In November 1923, in the city of Munich, Hitler attempted an armed takeover. This has become known as the Munich or **Beer Hall Putsch**, as the Nazis kidnapped three leading politicians who were meeting in a local beer hall ('putsch' is a German word for violent uprising).

Children use bank notes as building blocks during hyperinflation, 1923; the notes were virtually worthless

The putsch was a failure, the leading Nazis were arrested, and Hitler was sentenced to five years in prison. However, the event won him massive publicity, and every word he spoke at his trial was reprinted in Germany's newspapers. Many of Germany's conservative politicians and judges sympathised with Hitler's views. In the end, he only served nine months in prison, and he used that time to write a biography and manifesto that summarised his core beliefs: **_Mein Kampf_** ('My Struggle').

What is Fascism?

Fascism is a political ideology of the extreme Right. At its core is an aggressive and intolerant nationalism, which glorifies the nation and its leader above all else. This nationalism almost always has a strong racist component: the national community is defined in terms of a specific ethnic group, with other ethnic groups having no true place in the nation.

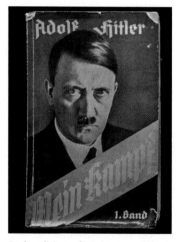

Early edition of *Mein Kampf*, first published in Germany in 1925

Check your understanding

1. What were the aims of the British and French leaders at the Paris Peace Conference?
2. What was the 'Stab in the Back' myth?
3. How was Hitler inspired by Italian politics?
4. What were the consequences of Hitler's first attempt to seize power?
5. Why did the Treaty of Versailles provoke so much anger and unrest in Germany?

The Great Depression

After the disasters of 1923, Germany entered a period of recovery, and ordinary Germans were at last able to live normal and peaceful lives again.

Much of the recovery was due to Germany's foreign minister, Gustav Stresemann. He became the leading Weimar politician, holding together a coalition of moderate left-wing and moderate right-wing parties to govern the country. He also introduced a new currency to end the hyperinflation. Most importantly, in 1924 he negotiated the **Dawes Plan**.

The Dawes Plan was an international agreement designed to help Germany pay its reparations while also rebuilding its economy. Under this plan, the United States lent Germany money that it could use to pay reparations. This money also went into rebuilding German infrastructure and helping businesses to expand, creating new jobs and raising living standards.

By 1928 Germany had recovered its pre-war status as the world's second-biggest industrial economy after the USA. However, the new prosperity was fragile, because it depended almost completely on US loans.

Gustav Stresemann (1878–1929)

Weimar culture

Germany in the 1920s was at the cutting edge of European culture. Nightclubs and cabarets in Berlin were filled with modern music and modern fashions, while German artists and filmmakers experimented with radical new styles. To conservative Germans, all these trends seemed **decadent**, proof of a decline in traditional moral values.

Economic disaster

In October 1929, the United States' stock market suddenly collapsed. The price of shares in major US companies dropped dramatically, in a financial disaster known as the **Wall Street Crash**. The crisis in the USA triggered a chain of economic crises all over the world, because so much of the world was connected to the US financial system through trade, loans and currency exchanges. The world was plunged into the **Great Depression**, the worst economic crisis in human history.

The Depression caused great suffering almost everywhere, as millions of people lost their jobs or lost their homes. It was particularly bad in Germany, because Germany was suddenly forced to repay its US loans, causing the economy to crash. Unemployment soon reached 6 million (over a third of the workforce), while wages dropped to less than two-thirds of their former level and production was almost halved. Millions of shops and businesses closed down, while the state was unable to provide money, jobs or even food for most of the unemployed.

Poster advertising the Wintergarten cabaret in Berlin in the 1920s

Faced with the Depression, the Weimar politicians seemed helpless. Desperate and struggling to survive, many Germans were pushed to support more extreme solutions.

The Nazis in the Depression

After his release from prison, Hitler had decided to try to win power democratically rather than attempting another putsch. The Nazis began campaigning for seats in the **Reichstag**, the German parliament. However, until the Depression hit, they remained a tiny fringe movement, winning less than 3 per cent of the vote in the 1928 election.

In the Depression, Hitler found a much wider audience was willing to listen to him. He blamed all of Germany's problems – from the current economic disaster to defeat in the war – on a number of groups he saw as unpatriotic domestic enemies: democrats, Socialists and Jews. He promised to restore German strength and pride, expel or destroy these 'enemies within', and rescue Germany from the Depression. Ordinary Germans flocked to the Nazis.

Hitler spread his message through the radio, the cinema and by giving speeches all over Germany. No politician had ever taken advantage of modern communications in this way before. Many conservative Germans also supported Hitler because they feared Communism, and felt that Hitler was the only politician tough enough to save Germany from a Communist takeover. In the election of July 1932, the Nazis' electoral support peaked at 37 per cent, making them the largest party in the Reichstag. However, they still did not have enough seats to form a government.

Hitler giving a speech in 1930

Hitler comes to power

In the Weimar political system, there was a President, who mostly stayed out of politics, and a Chancellor, who ran the government. On 30 January 1933, President Hindenburg reluctantly appointed Hitler as the Chancellor of Germany. This was part of a plot by the conservative Hindenburg and other right-wing politicians, who wanted to restore the pre-First World War authoritarian system. They believed that by bringing Hitler into government as part of a coalition with other right-wing parties, they could harness his popular support to advance their own agenda. The old conservatives were confident they could control Hitler. However, by making Hitler Chancellor, they handed him power that he would use to destroy not only them, but the entire existing order in Germany.

Check your understanding

1. How did the Dawes Plan allow Germany to recover in the mid-1920s?
2. What were the effects of the Great Depression in Germany?
3. What new political tactics did the Nazis employ when campaigning?
4. Why did President Hindenburg appoint Hitler as Chancellor in January 1933?
5. How did the Great Depression facilitate the rise of the Nazis?

The Third Reich

Within six months of being appointed Chancellor, Hitler had used his position to concentrate all political power in the hands of the Nazis.

The Nazi takeover

On 27 February 1933, there was a mysterious arson attack on the Reichstag building. Hitler blamed the Communists and said that the **Reichstag fire** showed that his government needed more power. Political opponents were arrested and imprisoned in their tens of thousands. All political parties besides the Nazis were banned, and government institutions throughout Germany converted themselves into Nazi institutions rather than be dissolved. A new law called the Enabling Act allowed Hitler to pass any law he wanted without going through the Reichstag or consulting Hindenburg. Hitler was now a fully empowered dictator.

When Hindenburg died in 1934, Hitler combined the roles of President and Chancellor and became known as the **Führer**, a German term that loosely means 'Leader'. His new German empire was called the **Third Reich**.

Life in Nazi Germany

After years of division and desperation, many Germans responded with great emotion to the Nazis' call for strength through unity, and to their radical rejection of the past. The Nazis appealed to the idea of a racial 'people's community' that could sweep away all divisions between classes and political parties, uniting all ethnic Germans in a spirit of national pride. Non-White Germans, including the Jews, would have no place in this new national community.

Poster of 1936, "All of Germany Hears the Führer with the People's Radio"

The Nazis engineered support through the masterful use of **propaganda**. Joseph Goebbels, Hitler's propaganda minister, was very skilful at using all possible media to manipulate popular opinion. All films screened in Germany had to have a pro-Nazi message, and newsreels promoting Nazi achievements were shown beforehand. Loudspeakers were placed on the street and in public bars so that everybody heard the Nazi radio broadcasts, while listening to a foreign radio service such as the BBC was punishable by death. Books that contained ideas that the Nazis deemed unacceptable were burned. Newspapers could print nothing anti-Nazi, and posters celebrating the Third Reich were plastered everywhere. The Nazi message was inescapable.

Most spectacularly of all, the Nazis held annual **rallies** in the city of Nuremberg. These were massive night-time events, lit with torches and featuring parades of marching

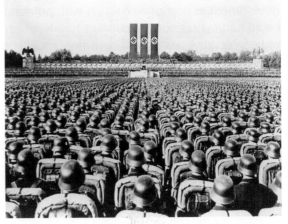

Nazi soldiers at the Nuremberg Rally, September 1936

troops, music and speeches by Hitler – all designed to inspire national pride and show off the power of the Nazi regime.

In school, children were taught a 'patriotic' version of German history that portrayed the Jews as constantly betraying the honest German people. Biology lessons taught that White Germans were racially superior to all other ethnic groups. Boys were encouraged, and eventually required, to join an organisation called the Hitler Youth, which trained them in outdoor activities while teaching them Nazi ideology. Girls were encouraged to join the League of German Maidens, which taught them that their duty as women was to stay in the home, support their husbands, and raise as many children as possible.

Meanwhile, Hitler was working constantly to prepare Germany for the next war. He planned to expand German territory by conquest in order to create 'living space' for the German people, principally in Eastern Europe. He therefore began a massive **rearmament** programme, manufacturing weaponry, planes and other military equipment. This broke the terms of the Treaty of Versailles, but it also had the useful side effect of bringing Germany back to full employment. Together with massive public works programmes to build railways, highways and houses, rearmament helped to stimulate a remarkable economic recovery.

A Hitler Youth poster of 1941: "Youth serves the leader"

The Berlin Olympics

Germany hosted the 1936 Olympics, and Hitler took the opportunity to show off the power of the Third Reich. He built a massive new stadium and used the media coverage of the games to broadcast Nazi ideology whenever possible. To the Nazis' embarassment, the Black US athlete Jesse Owens won four gold medals and became the star of the games, undercutting their pronouncements about the racial inferiority of Black Americans.

The police state

Obedience to the Nazis was enforced by a ruthless network of spies and police. A secret police agency called the **Gestapo**, led by Reinhard Heydrich, spied on the population and could arrest anybody, at any time, for any reason. Many people arrested by the Gestapo ended up in **concentration camps** for political prisoners. Conditions in these camps were horrific, and many prisoners died from beatings, overwork or random executions and torture.

The camps were run by an organisation called the **SS** (*Schutzstaffel*), meaning 'protection squad'. Orginally Hitler's private bodyguards, the SS had grown into an army of elite, ideologically driven Nazi agents. Under their commander, Heinrich Himmler, they were responsible for enforcing Nazi ideology and eliminating potential enemies of the regime. There was also a military division of the SS that operated within the army, known as the Waffen-SS.

Fact

Around 1.3 million Germans spent at least some time in concentration camps between 1933 and 1939.

Check your understanding

1. How did the Nazis use the Reichstag fire as an excuse to claim more power?

2. How were children in Nazi Germany raised to accept Nazi beliefs?

3. What additional benefits did Germany gain from Hitler's rearmament programme?

4. How did the Gestapo and the SS police the Third Reich?

5. How did the Nazis attempt to ensure that the people of Germany supported them?

Unit 3: Germany and the Nazis
Jews in the Third Reich

At the heart of Nazi ideology was a vicious anti-Semitism. Jewish people had lived in Germany for over a thousand years, but Hitler regarded them as a 'corruption' within the national community.

Hitler believed that White Germans represented the ideal racial type, which he called the '**Aryan race**'. He thought that the Jews, who never made up more than 1 per cent of the German population, were the greatest threat to the Aryan people. In Hitler's paranoid imagination, Jews were responsible for everything from anti-nationalist views in the Weimar press, to poor wages for working people, to trends in modern art that Hitler thought degenerate. He believed that the Jews controlled both Communism and international high finance, and that they had been responsible for the 'Stab in the Back' at the end of the First World War. In Hitler's worldview, the Jews were like a disease in the body of the German people, poisoning the racial community from within.

These views were not unique to Adolf Hitler – or even to Germany. Extreme anti-Semitism was common in Europe in the first half of the 20th century, and so the Nazis' message of hate fell on fertile ground. Anti-Semitism had many roots. It was partly religious, as Jews were blamed for the death of Jesus Christ; and partly economic, as some well-educated and successful business owners were Jewish, so they inspired jealousy in others. Yet ultimately, like all racism, it was irrational and lacked any logical justification.

The persecution of Jews

In the Third Reich, Jews experienced a slowly escalating persecution from the moment Hitler came to power. They were gradually stripped of their rights and excluded from mainstream German society.

In 1933, Jews were excluded from the civil service. They were also banned from a range of professions, including teaching. Soon afterwards, the Nazis began systematically forcing Jews out of their homes and businesses, driving many to emigrate from Germany altogether – though this could be difficult, as many countries would not accept them. As part of this process, Jewish shops were marked with a Star of David, and the German people were discouraged from shopping in them.

A Jewish man wears a Star of David, Germany, 1941

Non-Jewish victims

Though the Jews held a central place in the Nazi ideology of prejudice, they were not the only group to be persecuted. Roma (gypsies), Jehovah's Witnesses, Black people, the mentally ill, the disabled, LGBT people, alcoholics, the homeless, repeat criminals and the unemployed all faced discriminatory measures.

Then, in 1935, came a pair of laws called the **Nuremberg Laws**. The Reich Citizenship Law declared that only ethnic Germans qualified for citizenship. Jews were instead classed as state subjects with no citizenship rights. The Law for the Protection of German Blood and German Honour forbade marriage and sexual relations between Germans and Jews. These two laws effectively created a two-tier society.

In 1938, all Jewish people were required to take the additional name 'Israel' (for men) or 'Sarah' (for women), to further mark them out as Jews. In that same year, Jewish children were expelled from state-run primary schools, and Jewish newspapers and other publications were banned.

The persecution of German Jews took its most violent form yet in the massive **pogrom** (anti-Semitic attack) that occurred on the night of 9 November 1938. It began after the killing of a German diplomat by a Jewish man in Paris. Rampaging Nazi mobs attacked Jewish property, burned synagogues, and killed and wounded hundreds of Jews. Around 20000 Jews were taken to concentration camps. Because of the smashed windows of Jewish homes and shops, this pogrom became known as **Kristallnacht** – the 'Night of Broken Glass'.

Windows of a Jewish-owned shop smashed during *Kristallnacht*

All of these events paved the way for the mass murder of Jews, known as the Holocaust, that would begin in 1941. It is important to realise that the Nazis did not immediately begin attempting to exterminate the Jewish people as soon as they came to power. Instead, there was a gradual process in which discrimination was slowly normalised, so that as time went on there were fewer and fewer people in Germany who were willing to oppose it.

The killing of the disabled

In 1939, the Nazis began committing their first organised, systematic murders. The victims were the physically or mentally disabled, who were regarded as a burden on society and a corruption of the German race. The Nazis described these people as "life unworthy of life". Parents of disabled children were encouraged to admit their children to special treatment wards, where they would be secretly killed. The so-called euthanasia programme was soon extended to adult mental asylum patients who were deemed unfit to live. They were killed in gas vans: ordinary vans that had been specially converted so that poisonous carbon monoxide exhaust fumes were pumped into a sealed inner chamber. This organised killing foreshadowed the much more far-reaching programme of systematic murder that was soon to follow, this time targeting the Jews.

Victims of 'Aktion T4', the Nazis' non-voluntary euthanasia programme to exterminate psychiatric patients

Check your understanding

1. How did Hitler regard the Jewish people?
2. What were the provisions of the Nuremberg Laws?
3. What happened on *Kristallnacht*?
4. Why did the Nazis begin systematically killing disabled people in 1939?
5. What were the main impacts of Nazi policy on German Jews up until 1939?

Unit 3: Germany and the Nazis
The road to war

As the 1930s went on it seemed more and more likely that Hitler would start another war. The British and French governments were forced to decide what they should do about it.

The Rhineland

In March 1936, Hitler stationed troops in the Rhineland, the region that had been made a demilitarised zone by the Treaty of Versailles. This was an open challenge to the treaty, but the British and French chose not to oppose it. Many felt that the Treaty of Versailles had been unfair, and that Germany had a right to restore its international status. Some politicians also feared that challenging Hitler's attempts to restore German strength could cause another European war, and so they felt they should not stand up to him. This policy became known as **appeasement**: giving Hitler what he wanted in the hope that this would stop him from going any further. In Germany, meanwhile, the remilitarisation of the Rhineland was widely seen as a triumph: a firm rejection, at long last, of the hated Treaty of Versailles.

By 1937, Germany had also formed an alliance with two other powerful anti-democratic nations: Italy and Japan. This became known as the **Axis**.

Munich

In 1938, Hitler embarked on an ambitious programme of territorial expansion around the borders of Germany. He began with Austria. This was a German-speaking country and many Austrians were enthusiastic about joining with Germany, so Austria was peacefully absorbed into the Third Reich by an act of union called the *Anschluss*.

German police enter Tirol, in western Austria, during the Anschluss of March 1938

Hitler's next target was Czechoslovakia, which he now began making plans to invade. Hitler claimed that he wanted only the Sudetenland, a mostly German-speaking border region of Czechoslovakia. In reality, he planned to take over the whole country. The Czechs were determined to fight back.

In a series of meetings with Hitler in September 1938, the British prime minister Neville Chamberlain tried to make a deal that would avoid war. Chamberlain was a firm believer in appeasement, and he thought it was worth making any sacrifice to avoid another massive war in Europe. He did not believe Hitler could be serious about most of the extremist views he expressed, and he thought he could deal with Hitler as an honourable fellow statesman. Eventually, in the German city of Munich at the end of September, Chamberlain and Hitler struck a deal. Hitler would **annex** the Sudetenland but leave the rest of Czechoslovakia alone. Hitler also promised that this would be his final territorial acquisition in Europe. This settlement, which was made without consulting the Czechs themselves, was known as the **Munich Agreement**. Returning to London, Chamberlain confidently declared that with this deal he had secured "peace for our time".

Of course, Hitler had been lying. In March the next year, he annexed most of the remainder of Czechoslovakia. The British were finally forced to accept that appeasement did not work, and only a military confrontation would stop Hitler from invading more and more of Europe.

> **Fact**
>
> Czech people still usually refer to the Munich Agreement as the 'Munich Betrayal'.

The Nazi–Soviet Pact

Hitler's next move astonished the international community. The Nazis hated Communism, and Hitler had repeatedly condemned the Soviet Union as one of Germany's greatest enemies. Yet on 23 August 1939, Hitler and Stalin shocked the world by signing the Nazi–Soviet Non-Aggression Pact, which bound them not to attack each other.

Hitler still intended to invade the USSR eventually, but he wished to avoid fighting a two-front war to the west and the east simultaneously, as Germany had done in the First World War. He therefore planned to turn on the Soviets only when he had neutralised all other threats. Until that day, the **Nazi–Soviet Pact** bought him time, and left him free to focus on other conquests in Europe without the fear of Soviet interference. As for Stalin, it seemed clear to him that Britain and France would never stand up to Hitler's aggression, so he believed that a pact with Germany was the only way to protect the USSR. Even so, he doubted that Hitler would really stick to the pact in the long term.

On his return to the UK from Munich, Neville Chamberlain proclaims "peace for our time"; in his hands he holds the agreement signed by Hitler

The invasion of Poland

One week after the pact was signed, on 1 September 1939, Hitler invaded Poland. This moment marked the beginning of the Second World War, and two days later, the British and French at last declared war on Germany. It was too late to save Poland itself, which was soon invaded a second time: from the east, by the Soviet Union. Stalin was taking advantage of his alliance with Hitler to seize the eastern half of the country for the USSR. The conquest of Poland took little more than a month, as the two dictators divided the country between their two empires. The British and French Allies, meanwhile, prepared to meet Hitler's next attack.

German troops watch the bombing of Poland's capital, Warsaw, by the German Luftwaffe, September 1939

> ### Check your understanding
> **1.** Why did the British and French choose not to oppose the remilitarisation of the Rhineland?
> **2.** Why did Neville Chamberlain believe he could make a deal with Hitler?
> **3.** How did Hitler ultimately break the agreement he made with Chamberlain?
> **4.** Why did Hitler and Stalin sign the Nazi–Soviet Pact?
> **5.** Why did it take so long for Britain and France to stand up to Hitler?

Unit 3: Germany and the Nazis
Knowledge organiser

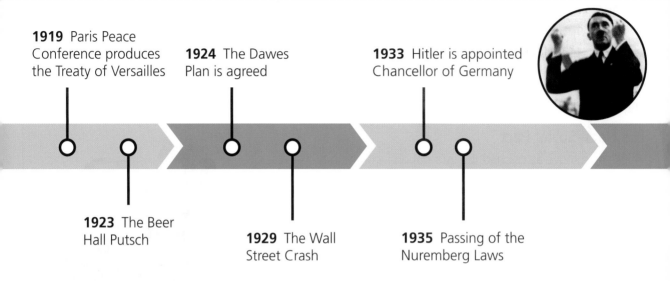

1919 Paris Peace Conference produces the Treaty of Versailles

1924 The Dawes Plan is agreed

1933 Hitler is appointed Chancellor of Germany

1923 The Beer Hall Putsch

1929 The Wall Street Crash

1935 Passing of the Nuremberg Laws

Key vocabulary

Anschluss Peaceful annexation of Austria by the Third Reich

Annex To take over a territory, usually by force

Anti-Semitism Prejudice and hatred of Jewish people

Appeasement British and French policy of allowing Hitler to take what he wanted in the hope that this would avoid war

Aryan race Imaginary ideal race that the Nazis believed White Germans represented

Axis Alliance between Nazi Germany, Fascist Italy and Japan

Beer Hall Putsch First attempt by Hitler to seize power; a violent uprising in the city of Munich in 1923

Concentration camp A camp where a government forces an enemy population to live

Dawes Plan International agreement in 1924 whereby Germany would borrow money from the USA in order to rebuild its economy and pay its reparations

Decadent In a state of moral decline, characterised by the indulgence of pleasures considered immoral

Fascism Political ideology based on nationalism, racism and intolerance of opposing ideas

Führer German term meaning 'leader,' used to refer to Hitler

Gestapo The secret police agency in Nazi Germany

Great Depression Severe worldwide economic collapse that lasted for much of the 1930s

Hyperinflation Massive rise in all prices that makes a currency useless and makes people's savings worthless

Kristallnacht Massive pogrom against German Jewish communities in 1938

Mein Kampf Book written by Hitler outlining his beliefs

Munich Agreement Agreement made between Hitler and Chamberlain allowing Hitler to annex part of Czechoslovakia in exchange for a promise to go no further

Nazi–Soviet Pact Agreement between the Third Reich and the USSR, stating that they would not attack each other

Nuremberg Laws Laws that stripped German Jews of citizenship and forbade them from marrying or having sexual relations with non-Jewish Germans

Pogrom Violent attack on a minority group, usually Jews

Propaganda Information or media that is designed to promote a particular ideology or set of beliefs

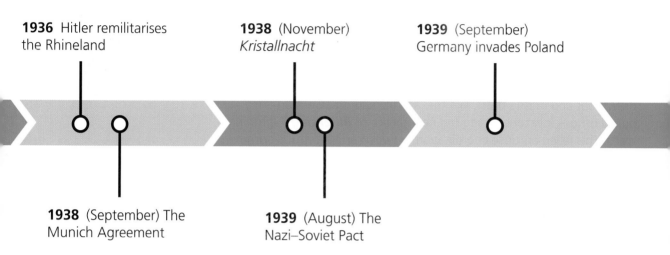

1936 Hitler remilitarises the Rhineland

1938 (November) *Kristallnacht*

1939 (September) Germany invades Poland

1938 (September) The Munich Agreement

1939 (August) The Nazi–Soviet Pact

Key vocabulary

Rally A mass gathering of people to show support for a political cause

Rearmament The process of increasing a country's armed forces again after a period of disarmament

Reichstag The German parliament, or the building in which it was housed

Reichstag fire Arson attack on the Reichstag that was used by Hitler as an excuse to seize more power

Reparations Payments made to make amends; often payments from a nation defeated in war to those who beat them

Rhineland Major industrial region of Germany that borders France

SS (Schutzstaffel) Elite organisation dedicated to enforcing Nazi policies

'Stab in the Back' myth Belief, held by many Germans, that Germany did not lose the First World War on the battlefield but was betrayed by domestic enemies

Third Reich Germany under the Nazis, meaning 'Third Empire'

Treaty of Versailles Treaty that formally ended the First World War and penalised Germany

Wall Street Crash Financial collapse in the United States that triggered the Great Depression

War Guilt Clause The section of the Treaty of Versailles that required Germany to formally accept responsibility for causing the war

Weimar Republic Democratic government of Germany between the abdication of Kaiser Wilhelm and the Nazi takeover

Key people

Neville Chamberlain British prime minister who supported appeasement

Joseph Goebbels Propaganda minister in Nazi Germany

Heinrich Himmler Head of the SS in Nazi Germany

Paul von Hindenburg President of Germany who appointed Hitler as chancellor

Adolf Hitler Leader of the Nazis and fascist dictator of Germany

Benito Mussolini Fascist dictator of Italy

Gustav Stresemann Leading German liberal politician and statesman of the 1920s

Unit 4: The Second World War
The war in Europe

In a series of rapid and devastating campaigns, the Nazi war machine took barely two years to bring almost all of Europe under Axis domination.

Most of Europe's military leaders expected this second war to be long, drawn out and mostly static, like the last. Instead, the German army pulled off quick victories using the new tactics of **Blitzkrieg** ('lightning war'). This relied on close coordination between artillery, truck-borne infantry and fighter planes, all moving at speed and mounting sudden, concentrated attacks. In the spring of 1940, Hitler seized Denmark, Norway, the Netherlands, Belgium and northern France. Greece and Yugoslavia followed in the spring of 1941.

The fall of France

Of all these campaigns, the most dramatic and shocking to the Allies was the conquest of France, which took less than six weeks in May and June 1940. The German army effectively sliced the Allied army in two, trapping 400 000 Allied soldiers in a small pocket of north-eastern France and Belgium. As the Germans closed in, nearly 340 000 of these men were desperately evacuated to Britain through the port of **Dunkirk**.

The evacuation of thousands of Allied troops from Dunkirk

If the Royal Navy's rescue operation had not been successful, Britain's capacity to continue fighting would have been severely limited.

Under the terms of surrender, around three-fifths of France, including its entire Atlantic and North Sea coast, was occupied by the Reich. The remainder of the country was allowed to remain theoretically independent under a conservative government based at Vichy. The **Vichy French**

North Africa

In June 1940, Italian forces based in Libya (an Italian colony) attacked British Egypt, with the goal of seizing the Suez Canal. For the next three years, the British and the Axis battled each other for control of the North African coastline. The desert war reached a turning point with British victory at the Battle of **El Alamein** in late 1942, which ended the Axis threat to Egypt. All Axis forces were finally expelled from Africa in May 1943.

regime actively cooperated with the Nazis for the rest of the war. This left Britain, under its new prime minister Winston Churchill, facing Germany almost alone.

The Nazi–Soviet war

With his control of continental Europe secure, Hitler felt free to turn his attention to the Soviet Union. On 22 June 1941, Hitler broke the Nazi–Soviet pact by marching 3 million German troops into the USSR in **Operation Barbarossa** – the largest invasion in human history. The Soviet Union joined the war on the Allied side, and the British (and later the Americans) found themselves in an uneasy alliance with the Communist dictator Stalin.

From its outset, the Nazi–Soviet war was characterised by destruction on an unprecedented scale. German soldiers were indoctrinated to view the people of Eastern Europe as racially inferior and to fear the Soviet Union as the source of a Jewish conspiracy to undermine German civilisation. They therefore indiscriminately burned towns, massacred civilians and exploited prisoners for hard labour.

Wartime propaganda poster featuring Stalin

At first the Germans won multiple victories, while the Soviet armies retreated in disarray. However, the *Blitzkrieg*'s reliance on rapid, constant movement and regular attacks proved impossible to sustain in the vast spaces of Russia. Not only that, Hitler had gambled on securing victory before winter, and so most of his troops were not supplied with winter clothing. As temperatures plummeted, rain dissolved the fields into mud, thick snow blocked the roads, and countless soldiers succumbed to frostbite. The German advance slowed and slowed.

In the first week of December, fighting in temperatures of −30°C, a German army failed to capture Moscow and was forced to a halt less than 50 kilometres from the city. With the failure to seize the capital, the momentum of the German invasion was lost. The Nazi–Soviet war now shifted into a prolonged attritional struggle, as German and Soviet armies wore each other down over years of brutal fighting. In such a war, the odds were stacked against Germany, which simply did not have the manpower reserves to continue pouring armies into the east. Stalin, on the other hand, could send army after army to fight the Germans, no matter how many Russians died. Over the coming three years, the effort to sustain the gruelling conflict with Russia would strain Germany to breaking point.

The Soviet death toll

Over 70 million people died in the Second World War. Around half of these were from the Soviet Union, including civilians. Accurate figures are very difficult to determine, but it seems that more than 10 million Soviet civilians were killed in German massacres or died of famine and disease when their homes were destroyed.

Check your understanding

1. How did the Germans achieve such rapid and decisive victories?

2. Why was the evacuation from Dunkirk so critical for Britain's war effort?

3. How was France governed following its surrender in June 1940?

4. In what ways did the Russian campaign present unique challenges to the German armies?

5. Why was the failure to achieve victory in Russia before winter such a disaster for the Germans?

Unit 4: The Second World War
The Holocaust

Between 1941 and 1945, the Nazis attempted to murder all the Jews of Europe. This genocide has come to be known as the **Holocaust**. Jewish people themselves remember it as the Shoah.

From the beginning of his dictatorship, Adolf Hitler had believed that the German community needed to be 'purified' by the elimination of what he regarded as 'Jewish racial poison'. However, by 1941 the German Reich had spread through Poland and into Russia, two countries with far larger Jewish populations than Germany. In cities that the Germans conquered, Jewish people were rounded up and forced to live in **ghettos**, sealed areas of their cities they were not allowed to leave. Living conditions in the ghettos were overcrowded and miserable, and many people died from disease and starvation. Jews were also required to wear a yellow **Star of David** that identified them as Jews – a policy extended to Germany itself in 1941.

When the Nazis invaded the Soviet Union, Hitler formed four SS killing squads, known as ***Einsatzgruppen***, to accompany the German armies into Russia and to slaughter all the Jews they found. These men would ultimately kill around 1.3 million Jews, mostly by firing squad. Often, Jews were rounded up and forced to dig their own mass grave, before being lined up along the edge of the grave and shot. It was expected that the remaining Jews in the Soviet Union would die from starvation and overwork under Nazi occupation.

The Final Solution

The killing of Jews on the eastern front was the beginning of the Nazi genocide. However, Hitler and the SS wanted a more systematic approach to exterminating the Jewish people. They developed a plan they called the 'Final Solution': they would establish a network of death camps in occupied Poland, where Jews would be killed not by bullets, but by the gas chamber. At a conference at Wannsee (a suburb of Berlin) on 20 January 1942, senior Nazi officials agreed to the mass **deportation** of Jews to the east. The **Wannsee Conference** set the number of Jews to be killed at 11 million. In the end the Nazis would kill 6 million.

Soon after Wannsee, a program of mass deportations to the new killing centres began. In all Nazi-occupied parts of Europe, Jews were rounded up by the **Gestapo** or by collaborating local police. They were told that they were being resettled in new communities in the east. Jewish people were packed onto trains like cattle, and sent away. During a journey that could take as long as 11 days, the Jews were given very little food or water and were constantly exposed to the elements. Many died before they even reached the camps.

Heinrich Himmler (left) and Reinhard Heydrich (centre), shown here in 1942, were the main architects of the Holocaust

Who knew about the Holocaust?

The Holocaust was never officially acknowledged by the Nazi government. In 1943, Heinrich Himmler, the head of the SS, told senior SS officers that the murder of the Jews was "a glorious page in our history that has never been written and cannot be written." Nevertheless, the Holocaust was a vast operation that required tens of thousands of bureaucrats, workers and soldiers to organise it. Many historians have concluded that the majority of ordinary Germans probably knew what was happening.

Resisting the Holocaust

In many ghettos across Eastern Europe, Jewish people put up armed resistance to their deportation. In most cases, these were people who knew they had no hope of surviving or escaping, and chose to die fighting rather than let themselves be taken to the death camps.

The biggest Jewish revolt against Nazi domination was the **Warsaw Ghetto Uprising**. The Warsaw ghetto was a tiny, squalid area of 3.4 square kilometres enclosed by a wall, where Jewish people had to survive on a basic supply of food and grain provided by the Nazi authorities. In the summer of 1942, deportations from the ghetto began, and the Warsaw Jews realised that they were being taken to their deaths. Some of them formed a secret resistance organisation called the Jewish Combat Operation (ZOB), commanded by a young resistance leader named Mordecai Anielewicz. Ghetto residents began constructing underground shelters in their basements.

On 19 April 1943, Himmler ordered the clearing of the ghetto and the deportation of all remaining Jews – perhaps around 40 000 of them. This was timed for Hitler's birthday the next day, but it also happened to be the eve of the Jewish festival of Passover. When German troops entered the ghetto, the ZOB sprang into action. They had only a small number of firearms and home-made bombs, but they kept up their resistance for almost a month. The Jewish fighters could strike quickly, then escape into the sewers or over the rooftops. The Germans were eventually forced to burn the ghetto and flood or smoke-bomb the sewers. But in the end, resistance was crushed, and the Warsaw Jews were either killed in action or transported to the death camps.

Jewish civilians are removed at gun point from the Warsaw ghetto by German SS soldiers, May 1943

Check your understanding

1. How did the Nazis treat the Jewish population in Poland when they took over the country?

2. What did the *Einsatzgruppen* do?

3. What was decided at the Wannsee Conference?

4. Why is it likely that many German people knew about the killing of the Jews?

5. How did many Jews resist deportation to the death camps?

The death camps

At the end of long journeys, trains full of Jewish prisoners from all over Europe would arrive in Poland, at camps built specially to kill them.

Of the six death camps, four existed only for murder: Treblinka, Belzec, Chelmno and Sobibor. At these camps, the vast majority of Jews would be killed in the gas chambers within a few hours of arrival. The other two, **Auschwitz** and Majdanek, were also slave labour camps. At Auschwitz, when the Jewish people arrived, they would be lined up on the platform at the railway station. An SS officer would walk down the line and select those who were fit for work, purely by glancing at them. The rest would go straight to their deaths.

Arrival of a train containing Jews deported to Auschwitz death camp in Poland

At the gas chambers, the victims were told they were going to be given a shower. All would strip naked, so that their possessions could be taken away. Then the Jews were ushered into large rooms with the word 'shower' marked clearly on the doors in all major European languages, and with fake showerheads on the ceilings. Once all of them were inside, the doors were locked. Through vents in the ceiling, a deadly gas was released into the room (carbon monoxide at most camps, though Auschwitz used a cyanide-based gas called Zyklon B). The gas took 15–30 minutes to kill everyone inside. It would have been a very painful death.

Units of Jewish prisoners called *Sonderkommandos* ('special units') would then remove the bodies from the gas chambers and take them to the giant crematoria to be burned. The entire killing process was industrialised, timetabled and designed for maximum efficiency, as though in a factory. All possessions of people brought to the camps were either burned or, more commonly, re-used for the German war effort. The *Sonderkommandos* even removed hair and gold teeth from victims so that these could be sent to be used in German factories. Hair was used to make textiles, or as stuffing for mattresses.

Life in the camps

Those prisoners who were kept alive to be used for slave labour had their heads shaved, their clothing removed, and were tattooed with a number. This number was now their only identity. Prisoners were put to work on a range of gruelling tasks including mining, brickmaking and construction. The camps also provided slave labour for factories run by German corporations, including the chemical manufacturing company IG Farben, which ran a factory at Auschwitz.

Fact

A tiny number of Jews escaped the death camps, including 667 from Auschwitz. When some of them managed to reach neutral countries, their reports helped to spread word of what was happening in Poland.

The slogan above the iron gates of Auschwitz read, 'Arbeit Macht Frei' ('Work sets you free'). In fact, the work done by inmates was designed eventually to kill them. Jews died from starvation, punishment beatings, exhaustion, torture or disease. Many were used for medical experimentation, which often meant they were operated on with no anaesthetic. Almost nobody in the camps survived for more than a year.

Late in the war, when it became clear that the Nazis were going to lose, deportations to the death camps were increased in a desperate attempt to kill as many Jews as possible while there was still time. Almost half a million Jews from Nazi-allied Hungary were sent to the camps in 1944 alone. Then, as the Soviet armies approached, Jewish prisoners were marched westward through the snow in massive death marches designed to kill them through exhaustion or exposure. Very few remained to be liberated when the Russians finally reached the camps.

The main gate of the concentration camp at Auschwitz, Poland

The banality of evil

In the history of the Holocaust, it is easy to find examples of extraordinary and obvious inhumanity. However, the vast majority of Germans who participated were not psychopaths, but average, law-abiding citizens, who took these jobs because they were convenient and who did not question or criticise what they were doing. Most Germans might not have actively supported the genocide, but they did not feel strongly enough to take a stand against it. In the words of the Italian chemist Primo Levi, one of the few who survived Auschwitz: "Monsters exist, but they are too few in number to be truly dangerous. More dangerous are the common men, the functionaries ready to believe and act without asking questions."

In 1961, the Jewish intellectual Hannah Arendt observed this phenomenon at the trial of Adolf Eichmann, a high-ranking Nazi who had been one of the key organisers of the Holocaust. Eichmann had been on the run, but he was finally captured and put on trial in Jerusalem. Arendt saw that he was not an obvious villain, but an ordinary, unthinking man who had committed horrific crimes simply because it was his job. Hannah Arendt called this the "**banality of evil**".

The Soviet army liberated the prisoners at Auschwitz in January 1945

Check your understanding

1. How were Jewish prisoners separated into groups when they arrived at Auschwitz?
2. What was the role of the *Sonderkommandos*?
3. What kinds of work did prisoners in the death camps do?
4. Why did so few Jewish prisoners remain in the camps when the Soviet armies reached them?
5. How did Primo Levi and Hannah Arendt interpret the psychology of the German people who participated in the Holocaust?

Unit 4: The Second World War
The war in Asia

Simultaneously with the war in Europe, a separate conflict was fought in East Asia and the Pacific. Here the aggressor was not Germany, but Japan.

Japan at this time was dominated by its armed forces. One of the leading generals, Hideki Tojo, even occupied the post of prime minister in order to directly dominate the government. Military policy was focused on nationalist expansion in East Asia. Tojo and his allies aimed to seize control of the region's resources and markets in order to make Japan the dominant Asian economic power.

In 1937 Japan had invaded China (see Unit 6, Chapter 2). By 1941, the Nationalist Chinese resistance seemed to be on the verge of defeat, and the Japanese generals and admirals could turn their attention elsewhere. They planned a massive campaign of conquest to bring huge swathes of Southeast Asia under their rule. The one great obstacle to this plan was the United States, which alone possessed the military might to oppose Japan in the Pacific. Admiral Isoroku Yamamoto, who was chief of the navy, insisted that before attacking its Asian neighbours, Japan should carry out a **pre-emptive strike** on the US naval base at **Pearl Harbor** in Hawaii.

Pearl Harbor

Pearl Harbor was the principal base of the American Pacific fleet. An attack on Pearl Harbor could destroy so many ships as to render the USA incapable of serious naval operations.

In the early morning of 7 December 1941, a force of 183 Japanese warplanes attacked the base, catching the Americans completely by surprise. A second wave of 170 warplanes attacked an hour and a half later. Dozens of ships and almost 200 aircraft were damaged or destroyed by bombing. Yet the attack, though devastating, did not go far enough. Many ships survived or were not damaged beyond repair.

US President Franklin D. Roosevelt had supported the Allies since the beginning of the war. However, he could not formally end the US policy of neutrality because of the strength of isolationist feeling among American voters. The attack on Pearl Harbor transformed this situation. With near-unanimous political support, Roosevelt declared war on Japan and on its ally, Germany.

The US economy was thoroughly reorganised for war. By 1943, factories were producing the same number of aircraft as had been destroyed at Pearl Harbor every two days. The sheer quantity of armaments that American industry could produce was enough to sustain the Allied war effort throughout the

The battleship USS *Arizona* sinking after being hit by the Japanese Pearl Harbor air attack

rest of the war. The longer the war dragged on, the more Germany and Japan struggled to secure sufficient resources and to maintain enough factories to produce the supplies necessary to keep on fighting. US economic power meant the Allies did not have this problem.

The Pacific War

After Pearl Harbor, Japan's wave of conquests rolled out according to plan. In the first six months of 1942 the Japanese brought one-sixth of the surface of the planet under their rule, easily capturing Hong Kong, Burma, Malaya, the Philippines, most of the Dutch East Indies, and the western Pacific Islands. The British colony at Singapore, a Royal Navy base regarded as one of the great fortresses of the empire, fell on 15 February when 140 000 soldiers and civilians were captured.

Japanese war crimes

Japanese treatment of prisoners of war was notoriously inhumane. This was partly due to a military code of honour that regarded surrender in any circumstances as shameful. In the eyes of many Japanese, Allied soldiers who had allowed themselves to be captured alive were dishonoured and unfit to live. Prisoners were routinely tortured, executed or worked to death, often while building railways and other infrastructure in the conquered territories. This was all in violation of internationally agreed codes of conduct for the treatment of prisoners of war.

The Statue of Peace, in Seoul, South Korea, commemorates victims of sexual slavery by the Japanese military during the Second World War

The new Japanese empire was officially called the 'Greater East Asian Co-Prosperity Sphere,' as the Japanese claimed to be liberating Asian peoples from their colonial masters. In reality, however, Japanese rule was often far more severe than European rule. Over 10 million civilians in China alone, and millions more in Southeast Asia, were forced into labour in which hundreds of thousands died. Up to 400 000 women, mostly Korean or Chinese, were forced to become sex slaves for Japanese soldiers. They were euphemistically known as '**comfort women**'.

Japanese expansion was finally halted at the naval Battle of **Midway** in June 1942, when American forces destroyed enough Japanese aircraft carriers and planes as to make further conquests unfeasible. The USA then began the painstaking process of reconquering the Pacific from Japan, one island at a time. Over years of bitter warfare, the frontiers of the Japanese empire were slowly pushed back.

Kamikaze

Late in the war, Japanese air force pilots began deliberately crashing their planes into US ships in order to cause massive damage. These suicide attackers were known as **kamikaze** pilots – a Japanese term meaning 'divine wind', named after the medieval storms that had saved Japan from invasion by the Mongols.

Japanese schoolgirls wave farewell to a Kamikaze pilot, Okinawa, Japan, April 1945

Check your understanding

1. What were the aims of Japan's military government in the 1930s and 1940s?
2. Why did Japan attack Pearl Harbor on 7 December 1941?
3. How did the USA combat Japanese expansion in Asia and the Pacific?
4. Why were Allied prisoners of war treated so brutally by their Japanese captors?
5. Why is the Japanese attack on Pearl Harbor often seen as a turning point in the Second World War?

Unit 4: The Second World War
The end of the war

By 1943, it was clear that Germany had reached the limits of its expansion and was on the defensive. Yet it would take another two and a half years before the Axis powers finally surrendered.

A second German offensive in the Soviet Union had culminated in a brutal five-month battle in the city of **Stalingrad**. When the German attackers surrendered in February 1943, the Nazis were forced to begin the long retreat from Russia. Soviet armies spent the next two years pushing them back to Germany.

The Battle of Stalingrad

The bombing of Germany

While the Soviets were advancing, the British sought to wear down the Germans through an airborne bombing campaign. Air Chief Marshal Arthur 'Bomber' Harris developed the controversial strategy of **carpet bombing**, destroying large urban areas, including some entire cities, in order to crush the morale of the civilian population. Around 400 000 German civilians were killed and almost 5 million left homeless by Allied bombing. The most damaging attacks used incendiary bombs to create massive firestorms that could reach 1600 °C. Historic German cities, including Hamburg and Dresden, were destroyed in this way.

The defeat of Germany

On 6 June 1944, code-named **D-Day**, a massive Allied invasion force landed on the beaches of Normandy. This was the product of over two years of secret and obsessively detailed planning by Churchill, Roosevelt and their generals. The man chosen to direct the invasion was the American Dwight D. Eisenhower, who was appointed supreme commander of the Allied Expeditionary Force in Europe.

The strategy for **Operation Overlord** relied on the use of overwhelming force to punch through the German coastal fortifications. Shortly after midnight on 6 June, thousands of parachutists were dropped into Normandy, tasked with destroying bridges and railways in order to prevent German reinforcements from reaching the coastline.

Breaking Enigma

German military communications were encrypted using an ingenious coding machine called **Enigma**. Breaking the Enigma codes would allow the Allies to track and anticipate the movements of German U-boats, thus protecting the trans-Atlantic supply lines on which the war effort depended. The Enigma codes were deciphered by a team led by the brilliant mathematician Alan Turing, working at **Bletchley Park**, the British code-breaking centre. After the war, Turing's electro-mechanical code-breaking machines became the foundation of computer science.

As dawn broke a fleet of 5000 ships began landing soldiers and tanks on five beaches (code-named Utah, Omaha, Gold, Juno and Sword), spread over an 80-kilometre section of the Cotentin peninsula. In a hail of machine-gun fire, men got out of their landing craft, often into deep water, and fought their way ashore through barbed wire and anti-personnel mines. Once on the beaches, they had to assault the concrete fortifications that the Germans had constructed to defend France's Atlantic coastline. It took the entire day, with the landings supported by intensive naval bombardment. By nightfall, all five beaches had been captured by the Allies.

From this foothold, the Allied armies could begin battling their way across Europe, liberating France before advancing into Germany. As the Red Army closed in from the east, Germany was squeezed between enemies on both frontiers. Vast areas of the country were physically wrecked, while hundreds of thousands of German soldiers died in a series of final, futile attempts to defend their homeland. On 30 April 1945, in a bunker beneath Berlin, Hitler committed suicide by shooting himself in the head. One week later, on 8 May, Germany surrendered unconditionally to the Allies.

American troops going ashore on D-Day

The defeat of Japan

In June 1945, the island of Okinawa, the last Japanese stronghold in the Pacific outside Japan itself, fell to the Americans after three months of fighting. The battle of Okinawa cost the lives of 108 000 Japanese and 12 000 American troops. By this point, a six-month campaign of aerial firebombing had destroyed dozens of Japanese cities. Japan retained control of parts of China and Southeast Asia, but their defeat was now clear.

A replica of the bomb that destroyed Nagasaki

Stalin had promised that he would declare war on Japan three months after the defeat of Germany. He was true to his word: in the early hours of 9 August, the USSR launched an invasion of Japanese-occupied Manchuria, Korea and Sakhalin. However, by this time, the USA had already delivered its own knockout blows.

The atomic bomb, the most destructive weapon ever invented, was developed during the last years of the war in a United States research programme called the **Manhattan Project**. In July 1945, the world's first nuclear bomb was detonated in the New Mexico desert. On 6 August, the USA dropped a nuclear bomb on the Japanese city of Hiroshima. Three days later, a second bomb was dropped on Nagasaki. To this day, these remain the only nuclear weapons ever to have been used in war. Several weeks later, on 2 September 1945, Japan surrendered.

The destroyer of worlds

The physicist heading the Manhattan Project, J. Robert Oppenheimer, said that when he witnessed the first nuclear explosion he recalled a line from the ancient Hindu text, the *Bhagavad Gita*: "Now I am become Death, the destroyer of worlds."

Check your understanding

1. What was the purpose of Arthur Harris' area-bombing campaign?
2. Why was it so vital for the Allies to break the Enigma codes?
3. What made the D-Day landings so challenging and so dangerous for the Allied armies?
4. How had the USA established dominance in the Pacific by mid-1945?
5. What new weapons did the USA use against Japan in August 1945?

Unit 4: The Second World War
Knowledge organiser

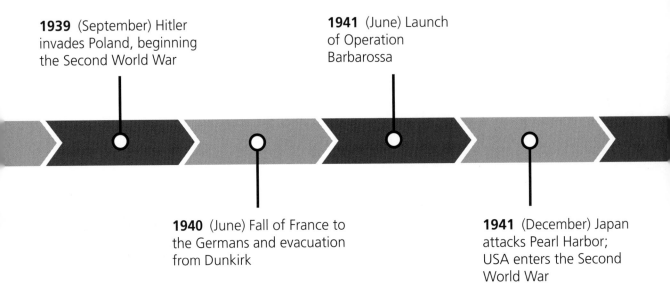

1939 (September) Hitler invades Poland, beginning the Second World War

1941 (June) Launch of Operation Barbarossa

1940 (June) Fall of France to the Germans and evacuation from Dunkirk

1941 (December) Japan attacks Pearl Harbor; USA enters the Second World War

Key vocabulary

Auschwitz Largest of the six Nazi death camps

Banality of evil The idea that ordinary people can commit war crimes if they are willing to uncritically follow orders

Bletchley Park The British code-breaking centre

Blitzkrieg 'Lightning war'; German term for warfare using fast-moving, mechanised units supported by fighter planes

Carpet bombing Also called area bombing, the strategy of bombing a large civilian area instead of specific military targets

Comfort women Term used by the Japanese during the Second World War to describe women kept as sex slaves for soldiers

D-Day Allied invasion of Nazi-occupied France

Deportation The forced removal of a person from a country

Dunkirk French port from which Allied troops were evacuated to Britain after the fall of France

Einsatzgruppen SS death squads that accompanied Operation Barbarossa in order to kill Jews

El Alamein (Battle of) Decisive battle of the North African war, when the British defeated Axis armies in Egypt

Enigma German coding machine used to encrypt military communications

Gestapo Nazi police, who rounded up Jews to deport them to the death camps

Ghetto An area of a city where Jewish people were forced to live

Holocaust Genocide of the European Jews by the Nazis

Kamikaze Japanese term meaning 'divine wind'; used to describe Japanese aircraft pilots who carried out suicide missions against US ships

Manhattan Project US research project that developed the first nuclear bomb

Midway (Battle of) Naval battle at which the USA inflicted enough damage on the Japanese fleet to prevent further conquests (a turning point in the Pacific war)

Enquiry Question: Which nation made the most important contributions to the defeat of the Axis: Britain, the USA or the USSR?

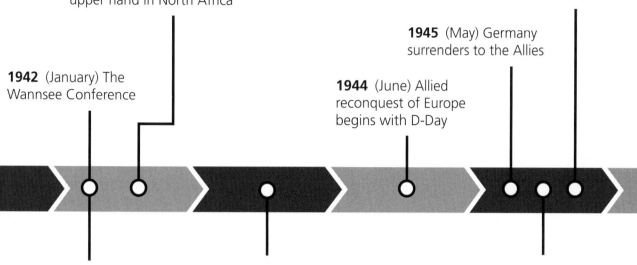

1942 (January) The Wannsee Conference

1942 (November) British victory at El Alamein gives the Allies the upper hand in North Africa

1944 (June) Allied reconquest of Europe begins with D-Day

1945 (May) Germany surrenders to the Allies

1945 (September) Japan surrenders to the Allies

1942 (June) Battle of Midway begins US reconquest of the Pacific

1943 (February) Battle of Stalingrad ends in Soviet victory

1945 (August) USA drops atomic bombs on Hiroshima and Nagasaki

Key vocabulary

Operation Barbarossa Hitler's invasion of the USSR in 1941

Operation Overlord Code name for the Allied invasion of Normandy in June 1944

Pearl Harbor United States naval base in Hawaii, headquarters of the Pacific fleet

Pre-emptive strike An attack carried out against an enemy before war has begun, in order to remove a possible future threat

Stalingrad (Battle of) Massive battle in the USSR (1942–3) that forced the Germans to begin retreating

Star of David A yellow six-pointed star that Jewish people were forced to wear to identify them as Jews

Vichy France Area of France under the pro-Nazi government that collaborated with Hitler

Wannsee Conference Conference in January 1942 at which senior Nazis agreed to the deportation of Jews to be killed in Poland

Warsaw Ghetto Uprising Armed resistance operation against deportation to the death camps that took place in the Warsaw ghetto

Key people

Hannah Arendt Jewish historian and philosopher who developed the concept of the "banality of evil"

Adolf Eichmann High-ranking Nazi who was a key organiser of the Holocaust

Dwight D. Eisenhower US general who commanded the Allied armies in Europe from D-Day until the end of the war, later a president of the USA

Arthur Harris Head of Britain's Bomber Command

Franklin D. Roosevelt President of the USA during the war

Hideki Tojo Japanese general and prime minister for most of the war

Alan Turing British mathematician who led the team that broke the Enigma codes and seen as a founder of computer science

Unit 5: Wartime Britain
Votes for women

At the beginning of the 20th century, very few women around the world had **suffrage** (the right to vote) and many were treated as second-class citizens.

The growth of factories in the 19th century meant that the range of jobs available to women broadened. In the UK by 1911, there were 600 000 women working in the textile industry alone. Other women worked as domestic maids and cooks, shop assistants or secretaries. However, it was still widely believed that men and women should occupy naturally different roles in life: men could be leaders, intellectuals and full-time wage-earners, while women were expected to stay at home raising children.

Early campaigns for women's rights

Although the 1868 Taunton Report had shown that girls and boys have equal mental capacities, many people still believed women's natures were 'irrational' and 'emotional'. Some thought that too much knowledge would make women 'unmarriageable' or affect their fertility, and so women's education was restricted. Others argued that women did not need suffrage as husbands or fathers could vote on their behalf. Many women, including Queen Victoria herself, believed that female involvement in politics went against traditional gender roles.

Early **feminist** campaigns successfully improved the provision of women's education and property rights. In Britain by 1864, 12 secondary schools for girls had been established, and in 1878 the University of London began awarding degrees to women. In 1882, married British women won the right to own their own property, which previously had been the automatic possession of their husband. However, equal voting rights with men still remained elusive. Then, in 1893, New Zealand became the first country in the world to give women the right to vote. This gave renewed hope to feminists in Britain for the suffrage cause.

The Suffragists

In 1897, Millicent Fawcett merged previous women's rights movements into the National Union of Women's Suffrage Societies (**NUWSS**), which became known as the **Suffragists**. Fawcett believed in winning the right to vote through peaceful demonstrations, logical argument in debates, writing petitions, and directly negotiating with politicians. The Suffragists argued that, as Parliament made laws that women were required to obey, women should have a say in making those laws. Despite risking their employment and reputations from being involved in NUWSS campaigns, by 1914 the NUWSS had over 100 000 members. However, none of the bills that the NUWSS persuaded politicians to introduce in Parliament were passed into law.

> ### Fact
> Una Dugdale sparked a national scandal in 1912 when she refused to say she would 'obey' her husband in her wedding vows. The marriage was not considered legal unless she did so.

A WOMAN'S MIND MAGNIFIED

Anti-suffrage posters attempted to make a mockery of women

The Suffragettes

Some women believed men would never consent to share power unless more direct means of rebellion were used. In 1903, Emmeline Pankhurst and her daughters broke away from the NUWSS and founded the Women's Social and Political Union (**WSPU**). Soon known as the **Suffragettes**, the Pankhursts published their own newspaper and held rallies across the country. On 21 June 1908, 30 000 women marched through the streets during the WSPU rally in Hyde Park, which attracted half a million spectators, making it the biggest demonstration the UK had ever seen. An exiled Sikh princess named Sophia Duleep Singh was crucial in funding the WSPU movement, and called for suffrage laws to change in the British colonies as well.

However, the WSPU also fought for the vote through bold publicity stunts under the slogan '**deeds not words**'. They chained themselves to buildings, disrupted political meetings, smashed windows, bombed mailboxes and set fire to empty buildings. Their increasing readiness to use more violent methods to secure suffragette goals alienated both men and women who might otherwise have been natural supporters of the cause, and the WSPU only had 5000 members at its height. Nevertheless, the Pankhursts' refusal to back down inspired great enthusiasm in their supporters across all sections of society, introducing a new mood of feminist militancy that MPs could not ignore.

A suffragette protest in London, 1908

More than a thousand women were arrested for participating in suffragette campaigns. In prison, many went on hunger strike to call attention to their cause. To stop these women from dying, which would have made them martyrs and won immense public sympathy, prison wardens brutally force-fed them. Another government response was to simply release hunger strikers until their physical condition improved and then re-arrest them. This was dubbed the '**Cat and Mouse Act**'.

Nonetheless, the suffragettes did gain a martyr in 1913 when Emily Davison was killed at the Epsom Derby while trying to attach a suffragette banner to the king's galloping horse. Cameras captured the shocking moment, which was published around the world, and thousands lined the streets for her funeral procession. However, soon afterwards, the outbreak of the First World War put suffrage campaigns on hold.

Fact

Edith Garrud was one of the first female martial arts instructors in the Western world. She trained suffragettes in jiujitsu to fight arrest.

Check your understanding

1. What rights had women gained through campaigns in the 19th century?
2. What were the main differences in methods between the NUWSS and the WSPU?
3. What did imprisoned Suffragettes do in order to call attention to their struggle?
4. How did Emily Davison call attention to the suffragette cause?
5. Were the NUWSS or WSPU more effective in gaining supporters?

Unit 5: Wartime Britain
The Home Front, 1914–18

During both world wars, the civilian population of Britain was expected to contribute to the war effort just as much as soldiers fighting overseas. This was known as the 'Home Front'.

In 1914, the Defence of the Realm Act (DORA) was passed. This established a policy of '**total war**': the whole of British society was mobilised for warfare by expanding industrial output to produce necessary armaments. As German submarine warfare reduced the volume of supplies reaching Britain, the early months of the war saw some panic-buying and hoarding of food. The government later introduced **rationing** for goods such as sugar and meat, and queues at shops became common.

Roles for women

On the outbreak of war, the NUWSS and WSPU paused their political protests and agreed to cooperate with the government. They promoted male enlistment and encouraged women to take up traditional male forms of employment to prove the worth of women as loyal citizens. Some women even went to the conflict overseas as ambulance drivers and nurses.

On the Home Front, over 2 million women volunteered to replace jobs left behind by men at war. From working in factories making uniforms, guns, vehicles and ammunition, to keeping farms, docks and transportation running, women were vital to the war effort. By 1918, 90 per cent of **munitions** factory workers, 4000 police officers, 117 000 transport workers and 260 000 farm labourers were female. Factory work was hard; it meant dealing with toxic paint fumes, 12-hour shifts and only one day off a fortnight, while also having to gather food from ration queues and look after children when at home. Women were also paid less than men under laws that protected male status at work.

Women working on a building site during the First World War

The number of women in employment rose from 24 per cent in 1914 to 37 per cent in 1918. At the same time, the types of jobs women were doing started to change attitudes about what women were capable of. Many jobs were physically strenuous or required technical skills, and some women even lost their lives. However, the new positions available to women were short-lived, as many lost their jobs when the men returned from fighting abroad after the war.

Air raids

Traditionally Britain's defence systems were focused on the navy and coastline. The country was ill-prepared to deal with the new threat of enemy airships and aircraft that had been developed in the early 20th century. At 11 000 feet, **zeppelin** airships could turn off their engines, drifting silently to carry out surprise bombing attacks in the night. In

January 1915, Britain experienced its first attack from the air, and there were a further 52 deadly zeppelin raids during the war. However, as zeppelins were filled with hydrogen gas they were highly explosive, so if searchlights could find them, anti-aircraft guns could shoot them down.

In May 1917, a new weapon that had not been used in war before was released to terrorise Britain. Twenty-one Gotha bi-plane bombers droned across the skies, each carrying 13 bombs and machine guns at the front and rear. By 1918, Germany had even developed Riesens ('Giants'), which were capable of dropping bombs 13 feet long and weighing a metric ton.

A German propaganda postcard circa 1916 showing a Zeppelin airship bombing London

Over 1400 people in Britain were killed in air raids during the First World War, and more than 3400 were wounded. This created great panic and anxiety among civilians in the cities. They feared going to work in the factories and docks, which were targets of the attacks, or even to spend the night in their homes. More than 300 000 people used the London Underground stations to shelter from German attacks (double the number of people sheltering at the height of the London Blitz in September 1940).

Pacifist movement

When war broke out in 1914, Britain relied on volunteers to enlist into the army. Propaganda aimed to stir patriotism and hatred of the enemy as well as personal shame and social isolation if men did not 'do their duty'. However, many people didn't place much trust in what they heard, and disagreed with the aims of the fighting.

In January 1916 the Military Service Act was passed, forcing all men aged 18–41 years into the armed forces (except priests, teachers, certain industrial workers and the medically unfit). This raised 2.5 million troops but was not popular. **Conscientious objectors** refused to fight on moral grounds, an attitude known as **pacifism**. More than 16 000 were taken to trial and refused exemption, while 6000 were sent to prison for resisting military authority. They were criticised before and after the war for their pacifist beliefs, and perceived as cowards rather than humanitarians.

International Congress of Women

Many women were devastated that their fathers, husbands, brothers and sons were being sent away to die. In 1915, 1136 women from around the world met in the Netherlands to discuss resolutions for a peace founded on gender equality, human rights and social justice.

Check your understanding

1. What did the NUWSS and WSPU do when war broke out?

2. Why did the types of roles women performed on the Home Front change attitudes towards women?

3. What types of air raids did Britain suffer during the First World War?

4. Why did some people decide to be conscientious objectors?

5. What was the most significant way the Home Front helped Britain win the First World War?

Interwar Britain

After the death and destruction that the First World War brought to Britain, the 1920s were a time of social experimentation.

Every single town and village in Britain had been affected by the war, and hardships and trauma remained. The younger generation wanted to be freer than their parents and to live life to the full, in memory of those who were lost.

Changes in popular culture

The experience of the First World War had brought people together and challenged traditional class and gender roles. In 1918, the **Representation of the People Act** gave universal suffrage to all men over 21 years (regardless of property ownership), thus ensuring that all working-class men could vote. The Act also gave about 40 per cent of women the right to vote, but only if they were over the age of 30 and met a middle-class property qualification. It took another decade of campaigning before the 1928 **Equal Franchise Act** gave all British women the same voting rights as men.

Aside from winning the suffrage campaign, the position of women also changed in other ways during the interwar years. Old Victorian moral and physical restraints were abandoned in favour of more freedoms. Middle-class women were now able to walk without chaperones in the street and could smoke, wear make-up and drink alcohol freely – older generations saw these new developments as immoral and labelled the women '**flappers**'. Women also cut their hair into short bobs and wore dresses that were loose and exposed their legs and arms.

New technologies also changed British life. By the 1930s, horse-drawn vehicles had practically disappeared from city streets, replaced by over 2 million motor cars. This was also the age of visual media as cameras and photography became cheaper. Cinemas were built to show new 'moving pictures' of the news, as well as cartoons and movies. By 1937, Hollywood movies shown in British cinemas were selling 946 million tickets per year. In addition, by 1939 there were 9 million radio sets in British homes. The radio became a powerful tool for giving information to the masses. Radio also popularised new music like jazz and blues of African-American origin, and people bought records and gramophones to own their favourite tunes.

Car ownership in the English suburbs in the 1920s

In 1918 the Education Act raised the school leaving age to 14 years for both boys and girls. This greatly expanded literacy, encouraging the publication of a wider and cheaper range of newspapers and magazines, as well as paperback fiction books from 1935 and comics from DC and Marvel by 1939. The increase of mass media led to a focus on celebrities, especially sports heroes and movie stars. Cities supported their home teams in huge sports stadiums, and the popularity of football increased with the first World Cup staged in 1930.

However, the glamorous perception of the 'roaring 20s' overshadows the deep social unrest that was also present. The UK economy was in decline after the war, and by the mid-1920s unemployment had risen to over 2 million, reaching 70 per cent in the north of England and Wales. In 1926, 1.7 million workers went on a **general strike** to protest against government wage reductions for coal miners. There was fear that a Communist revolution might begin, as had happened in Russia in 1917 (see Unit 2, Chapter 2).

The British Union of Fascists

Britain was also not immune to the rise of fascism that swept across Spain, Italy and Germany. In schools, children were taught that White British people deserved to be rulers over others in the empire. The Eugenics Education Society was set up in London in 1907 to promote the study and 'improvement of race', while the government passed the Aliens Act in 1905 to deny entry to 'undesirable immigrants' (aimed at Eastern European Jews).

In 1932, a politician named Sir Oswald Mosley created the British Union of Fascists (**BUF**). A persuasive speaker, Mosley used racist ideas and anger over economic decline to propose a single-party authoritarian regime. Their black uniforms, salutes and rallies mirrored the rise of the fascists elsewhere, and the BUF grew to perhaps over 50 000 members. In 1936,

Oswald Mosley leads a BUF rally in London, 1937

the BUF organised a march through London's East End to intimidate the Jewish population living there. However, anti-fascist demonstrators blockaded the roads and fought BUF members to stop them marching through. This became known as the Battle of Cable Street and was seen as a victory against rising anti-Semitism in Britain.

> ### Fact
> The British Broadcasting Corporation (BBC) was created in 1922. Its purpose was "to inform, educate and entertain".

> ### Prohibition
> In 1919, US politicians decided to prohibit (ban) the manufacture, import and sale of alcohol entirely, as a way to avoid the health and social issues it causes. However, criminal mafia gangs started to make their own alcohol and sell it illegally at underground clubs called 'speakeasies', famous for their jazz and cocktails. This led to an increase in gang violence and corruption and the law was repealed in 1933. With this, the cause for British **prohibition** laws was lost.

Check your understanding
1. What new freedoms did women gain in the 1920s and 1930s?
2. What new technology was developed in the 1920s and 1930s?
3. What social unrest was still evident in the 1920s?
4. What did Sir Oswald Mosely try to do?
5. What was the most significant change in popular culture in the interwar years?

Unit 5: Wartime Britain
Churchill and the Battle of Britain

With France defeated and Britain's troops evacuating from Dunkirk in 1940, Hitler was in a prime position to invade and conquer Britain.

The Nazi plan to invade Britain was known as **Operation Sealion**. Before any invasion could be launched, they needed to subdue the British Royal Air Force (**RAF**) and secure supremacy in the skies. Germany planned to destroy the RAF in order to allow the **Luftwaffe** (German air force) to drop paratroopers, secure ports and allow Panzer tank divisions to be shipped over to south-east England. The same Blitzkrieg tactic that had made Nazi Germany the unquestionable dominant power in mainland Europe could then be used to conquer Britain. Hitler hoped that Britain would quickly accept his offer of a peace agreement, but the new Prime Minister would not back down without a fight.

Churchill as Prime Minister

Winston Churchill is widely remembered in Britain as a great war-time prime minister. However, his appointment at the head of a cross-party coalition on 10 May 1940 was controversial. Churchill was 65 years old and his career up to this point had been subject to widespread criticism. He was seen as a rogue politician who had switched political parties, directed the failure at Gallipoli in the First World War (see Unit 1, Chapter 4) and staunchly opposed Indian independence; he was a committed supporter of British imperialism, and was widely seen as a war-monger. Much of the nation, including the royal family, preferred Churchill's rival Lord Halifax, the Foreign Secretary.

Winston Churchill (1874–1965)

However, Churchill had spent the 1930s opposing Neville Chamberlain's policy of appeasement and warning of the threat posed by Hitler. His energy and steadfast determination to keep fighting (when others such as Halifax wanted to negotiate a peace settlement to avoid further death and destruction) made Churchill an iconic symbol of resilience. He inspired the nation by the power of his rhetoric, his speeches helping to maintain British morale. In perhaps his most famous speech, given after the **evacuation** from Dunkirk, Churchill declared: "We shall fight on the beaches, we shall fight on the landing grounds, we shall fight in the fields and in the streets, we shall fight in the hills; we shall never surrender."

The Battle of Britain

In July 1940, the Luftwaffe had 2800 planes, almost four times as many as the RAF. It seemed the perfect time to launch the air offensive. Between July and October 1940, the **Battle of Britain** was fought out in the skies above southern England – mostly over a region of Kent called 'Hellfire Corner', the area of Britain closest to the German-controlled airfields in Europe. This was the first major campaign ever to be fought entirely by air forces.

While the Luftwaffe had a higher number of planes, the bombers were large and slow and were poorly protected by fighter planes that often needed to leave the fight to refuel. In comparison, the British had around 900 fighter planes called Spitfires and Hurricanes. The Spitfires were amazingly fast and proved deadly against the German bombers. Nearly 3000 men of the RAF took part in the Battle of Britain. While most of the pilots were British, men came from all over the Commonwealth, as well as volunteers from occupied Europe such as Belgium, France, Poland and Czechoslovakia. Unlike the Germans, these men were fighting to keep Britain free, and fighting for the future of their own countries. The average age of the British pilots was just 20 years old.

Nonetheless, a key reason for the successful defence of Britain was the recent invention of **radar**. A network of radar stations was able to precisely detect the numbers, position and direction of incoming German planes, while real-time communication with RAF fighters in the air via radio allowed them to accurately intercept the enemy squadrons. This system meant that the British would be aware of an attack an hour before the Germans arrived, giving them time to prepare their defences. The Luftwaffe also failed to identify aircraft production centres and halt the creation and repair of more RAF planes.

By mid-autumn, British pilots and radar operators had together ensured that British airspace would remain under British control. The Luftwaffe did not succeed in defeating the RAF. Instead, Hitler changed tactic and decided to bomb Britain into submission while turning his attention back to mainland Europe. Winston Churchill declared: "Never in the field of human conflict was so much owed by so many to so few."

RAF pilots run to their spitfires during the Battle of Britain, 1940

The Home Guard

The concern of a Nazi invasion led to the creation of the **Home Guard**. This was made up of men between 17 and 65 years who were:

- older, injured or retired soldiers who had served in the First World War or had fought in the Spanish Civil War in the 1930s
- young men not yet conscripted
- those in reserved occupations such as farmers, dockworkers, miners, teachers and doctors.

Their role was to act as a secondary defence force if Britain was invaded. 1.5 million men signed up and their roles were important for operating anti-aircraft guns during the Battle of Britain, as well as helping inspect unexploded bombs or rescuing people from bomb damaged buildings.

Check your understanding

1. What did Hitler's Operation Sealion involve?

2. Why was Winston Churchill's appointment as British Prime Minister in 1940 controversial?

3. Why were the Luftwaffe at a disadvantage to the RAF?

4. Why was the invention of radar significant?

5. What was the most important reason for the British victory in the Battle of Britain?

Unit 5: Wartime Britain
The Home Front, 1939–45

In the Second World War, Britain was under serious threat of invasion from Nazi Germany, so strengthening the Home Front was of even more vital importance.

Just as in the First World War, the British government imposed a policy of total war, with all areas of society mobilised to help the war effort. This meant higher taxes and longer working hours. Strict rationing was introduced for all staple foods except potatoes and bread. Ration books allocated how much each person could have of each rationed food, and spare land such as local parks and playing fields were dug up to grow more.

The **Ministry of Information** was the government department tasked with controlling news and communication with the public. Posters and leaflets were published with information about how to behave appropriately to support the country. News items that were thought to bring down morale were censored in the press, and private letters were even opened and redacted with thick black lines crossing out text.

The National Service Act of 1941 legalised the conscription of all men under 50 and all women under 30 into government-assigned war work. By 1943, 7.25 million women were working in roles such as mechanics, engineers, munitions workers, air-raid wardens, telephone operators and fire engine drivers. Some 80 000 women worked in the Women's Land Army ensuring farms were kept running, and 640 000 worked in the women's auxiliary units of the army, navy and air force abroad. However, as with the First World War, when men returned from fighting abroad, women were pushed out of these positions and forced to conform to more traditional gender roles in the home.

Evacuation

With advancements in aircraft technology and the experiences of the First World War, the government expected that Britain's large industrial areas would come under heavy bombing attacks. In September 1939, the evacuation of 1.5 million children from major cities to the countryside began.

An evacuee's experience would differ hugely depending on where they were based and who they lived with. Many children had happy experiences with their host families, learning new things in a new environment and making new friends. However, others had very bad experiences. They came with few clothes and their host families did not look after them well; some children were beaten, abused or even made to work. For many children it was difficult to adjust to country life with no idea when they might return home. Homesickness was common, and many children were orphaned after their parents died in the bombing raids.

> ### Official government packing list for evacuees
>
> One vest, one pair of pants, one shirt with collar, one jersey, one pair of trousers/dress, handkerchiefs, two pairs of socks, pyjamas, comb, towel, face cloth, toothbrush, boots, coat, gas mask, identity card, egg or cheese sandwich, nuts and raisins, dry biscuits and cheese, barley sugar, an apple or orange.

Evacuee children at a Birmingham railway station, September 1939

The Blitz

From 7 September 1940 to 11 May 1941, the Luftwaffe launched 71 major bombing raids on London and dozens more on other cities including Coventry, Bristol, Birmingham, Glasgow and Liverpool. This was the bombing campaign known as the **Blitz**. Hitler's aim was to break morale and destroy strategic points such as railway lines, factories and docks. He was convinced that Britain would surrender to avoid more destruction.

People swiftly grew used to the sound of air-raid sirens, while every night a blackout was imposed to ensure no lights presented a visible target to the bombers above. People hid and slept in bomb shelters built in public squares or private gardens as well as cellars and London underground stations.

In 1944, the Germans developed **V-1** flying bombs (known as 'doodlebugs' from the sound they made) and **V-2** rockets. These were pilotless missiles fired at Britain directly from launch sites in Europe, making them deadly and almost impossible to prevent. In total, over 60 000 British civilians died during the bombing raids, with thousands more seriously injured. Many people lost their homes and possessions – in London alone, 116 000 houses were destroyed and another 2 million were damaged, while major landmarks such as Coventry Cathedral were destroyed. However, Britain did not surrender and Hitler was never able to launch his land offensive as planned.

A German bomber flying over London

Fact

On the first day of the Blitz in London, a fire spread that is estimated to have caused more damage than the Great Fire of 1666.

Fact

The Home Guard constructed over 600 underground bases across Britain. In the event of Nazi occupation, Home Guard units would be instructed to hide underground and secretly destroy supply lines, disable vehicles and assassinate Nazi officers with sniper rifles.

Tube stations in London doubled as air-raid shelters

Check your understanding

1. What did the Ministry of Information do during the Second World War?
2. How did women become involved in war work during the Second World War?
3. Why were children evacuated from cities?
4. How much destruction did the Blitz cause?
5. In what ways did the Home Front during the Second World War differ from the First World War?

Knowledge organiser

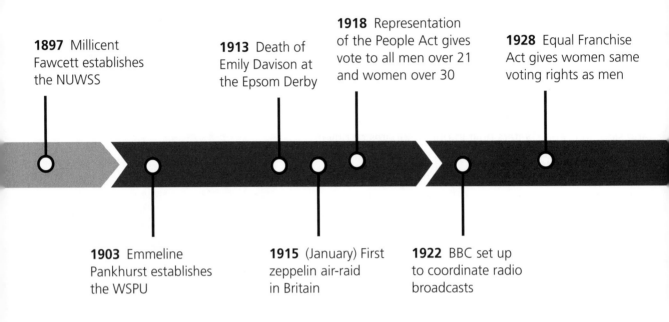

1897 Millicent Fawcett establishes the NUWSS

1913 Death of Emily Davison at the Epsom Derby

1918 Representation of the People Act gives vote to all men over 21 and women over 30

1928 Equal Franchise Act gives women same voting rights as men

1903 Emmeline Pankhurst establishes the WSPU

1915 (January) First zeppelin air-raid in Britain

1922 BBC set up to coordinate radio broadcasts

Key vocabulary

Battle of Britain German attempt in 1940 to gain control of British airspace in order to prepare for an invasion.

Blitz Bombing of Britain by the Germans

BUF British Union of Fascists

Cat and Mouse Act Name given to the 1913 government response to suffragettes on hunger strike to release them until well and then re-arrest

Conscientious objectors People who refuse to fight in a war on moral grounds

Deeds not words Slogan of the WSPU

Equal Franchise Act Passed by Parliament in 1928 to give women equal voting rights with men

Evacuation Process of moving children away from major cities to avoid bombing raids

Feminist A person who supports women's equal rights with men

Flappers Name given to the more free and independent young women of the 1920s

General strike When workers in multiple industries strike at the same time

Home Guard British citizen militia to help defend Britain against Nazi invasion

Luftwaffe The German air force

Ministry of Information Government department in Second World War that censored the news and created posters and leaflets

Munitions Military equipment

NUWSS National Union of Women's Suffrage Societies; also known as the Suffragists

Operation Sealion Hitler's plan to invade and conquer Britain

Pacifism The belief that war and violence are always unjustifiable and disputes should be settled peacefully

Prohibition Period from 1919 to 1933 in the USA when alcohol was banned

Radar Technology that locates and tracks objects by bouncing radio waves off them

RAF Royal Air Force, the British air force

Rationing Government control of goods and foods giving each person a fixed amount

Representation of the People Act Passed by Parliament in 1918 giving men over 21 and women over 30 the right to vote

Enquiry Question: What changed people's lives the most in the first half of the 20th century?

1932 British Union of Fascists (BUF) established by Sir Oswald Mosely

1940 (May) Winston Churchill becomes Prime Minister of Britain

1940 (September) The Blitz begins

1939 (September) Children begin to be evacuated from cities

1940 (July) Battle of Britain begins

Key vocabulary

Suffrage The right to vote

Suffragists Name for non-militant NUWSS

Suffragettes Name for militant WSPU

Total war Policy of mobilising an entire society and economy for a war effort

V-1, V-2 German pilotless missiles fired at Britain from Europe

WSPU Women's Social and Political Union; also known as the Suffragettes

Zeppelin Hydrogen filled airship that was used as a form of transport and for bombing raids

Key people

Winston Churchill British Prime Minister during the Second World War

Emily Davison Suffragette killed at the Epsom Derby

Millicent Fawcett Founder of the National Union of Women's Suffrage Societies (NUWSS)

Sir Oswald Mosley Founder of the British Union of Fascists (BUF)

Emmeline Pankhurst Founder of the Women's Social and Political Union (WSPU)

Unit 6: Modern China
The Chinese Nationalists

In 1911, the Chinese Empire collapsed, and over 2000 years of rule by the emperors came to an end. There was no agreement on who should replace them.

A Chinese **Nationalist** movement had existed for many years, hoping to create a Chinese Republic that would be democratic and progressive. Its leader was Sun Yat-Sen, a doctor and Christian convert who had lived for years in Japan attempting to direct a revolution from abroad. However, on 10 October 1911, when revolt broke out among army officers in the city of Wuhan, Sun was not involved – he was fundraising in the United States. Sun had to hurry home, while this unexpected rebellion spread rapidly through the country.

The rich gentry sided with the army against the imperial government, and it was clear that the ruling Qing dynasty had lost control. In December, Sun Yat-Sen and the Nationalists declared a provisional Chinese Republic, with its capital at Nanjing and Sun as president. The last emperor, a boy named Puyi, abdicated a few months later. However, Sun's government was weak, with few sources of revenue and little support from the mass of the people or the military. Sun was soon forced to give up the presidency to a popular army general named Yuan Shikai, who then blocked any moves towards parliamentary democracy. A few years later, Yuan himself lost control, as other generals based in different provinces competed for power. By 1916, China had fragmented into a collection of territories ruled by **warlords**.

Sun Yat Sen, Provisional President of the Republic of China from 1 January to 10 March 1912

For the next 10 years China was officially a republic, but in reality there was no central authority. Most of the warlords had little interest in improving the country or encouraging development, so most Chinese people continued to live as peasants. Living standards were very low: China had very little industry or railway track in 1920, and in some provinces up to 40 per cent of the population lived in poverty.

During these years, the Nationalists formed a new base in the city of Guangzhou (Canton) in the far south, one of China's most progressive and modernised cities, with strong links to the West. Here they organised themselves into a new political party, the **Guomindang (GMD)**. The Nationalists also began working closely with another new political group, the **Chinese Communist Party (CCP)**. The Communists shared the GMD leadership, and the two parties formed a common front for the reunification and modernisation of China.

Chiang's Northern Expedition

It would take a new leader for the Nationalists to acquire real power in China. In 1925, Sun Yat Sen died, and leadership of the GMD passed to Chiang Kai-Shek, the head of the small Nationalist army. Chiang was a hot-headed man who had previously belonged to an underground criminal organisation, with which he maintained close ties. He was also intelligent, ambitious, and an effective leader.

In July 1926, Chiang launched a massive military expedition to the north, declaring that he intended to complete the national revolution. The **Northern Expedition** lasted for two years, and eventually succeeded in reuniting all of China. Chiang's forces were smaller than most of the armies of the warlords, but they were disciplined and extremely well trained, and they increasingly gained the support of ordinary Chinese people who saw the GMD as a force for peace and reform. Chiang was also very good at securing alliances with key business leaders in Shanghai, who gave him financial support. By 1928, Chiang had defeated or made deals with all the warlords and established a new Chinese Republic with himself as president. This time, Nationalist control was real, backed by military strength and recognised across most of the country.

Chiang Kai-Shek (1887–1975), President of the Republic of China

However, Chiang's power was still not secure, because in the process of reunification, he had made an enemy of the Nationalists' old political partner. Chiang mistrusted Communism and feared that the CCP would hold too much power if they were part of his new republican government. In 1927, while the Northern Expedition was still underway, Chiang launched a series of brutal purges against his Communist allies. In multiple cities, thousands of Communists and labour union members were massacred, with many being beheaded in the streets by Nationalist troops. From this point on, Communists and Nationalists were bitter enemies. The Communist leaders retreated into the countryside and bided their time.

Chiang's regime also faced a second powerful enemy, not within China but across the sea: the expanding power of Japan.

Pronouncing Chinese names

In the **Pinyin** transliteration system (the standard way of writing the Chinese language using the Western alphabet), these rules apply:

- 'Q' is pronounced like the 'ch' in *charm* or *chocolate*.
- 'X' is pronounced like the 'sh' in *shirt* or *shallow*.
- 'Zh' is pronounced like the 'j' in *jam* or *jet*.
- 'Ou' is pronounced like the 'o' in *go* or *hippo*.

It is important to know that in Chinese names, the surname is given first. For example, in the name Sun Yat-Sen, 'Sun' is the family name and 'Yat-Sen' is the personal name.

Check your understanding

1. How did the Qing emperors of China lose control of the country?
2. Why did the government founded by Sun Yat-Sen in 1911 fall apart so quickly?
3. How was China reunited under Nationalist rule in the late 1920s?
4. Why did Chiang Kai-Shek turn against the Chinese Communists in 1927?
5. Why was Chiang Kai-Shek so much more successful than Sun Yat-Sen as a Nationalist leader?

Unit 6: Modern China
Nationalist, Communist, or Japanese?

The Guomindang government was corrupt and undemocratic, and it failed to transform China into a successful modern nation.

Chiang never introduced elections, and ruled instead as a military **autocrat**. Those who criticised his regime risked being imprisoned and tortured by his police force. There were some serious efforts to modernise the country, but progress was very slow: in a population of 450 million, only half a million children went to secondary school, and there were only 5000 doctors for the whole country. Many of the GMD's reforms were also ignored in practice: for example, though child labour in factories was banned, it remained extremely common. Government officials preferred to take bribes from criminals or businessmen rather than enforce the law.

In the 1930s, China was also under constant threat from the Japanese. Japan at this time was controlled by a military dictatorship focused on territorial expansion. In 1931, the Japanese army annexed **Manchuria**, the rich and industrially developed north-eastern region of China. To rule Manchuria on their behalf, the Japanese brought in Puyi – the last emperor, who had grown up hating the Nationalists. In the years that followed, Japan repeatedly threatened to seize even more Chinese territory.

Emperor Puyi in Beijing, 1932

The Communists

With Chiang distracted by Japan, the Communists built up their support among the rural peasants. The original leaders of the CCP had been discredited by the failure of their collaboration with the GMD. A new group of top officials now emerged to replace them. There was Zhou Enlai, an intellectual Marxist who had studied in Paris; Lin Biao, a brilliant general who had won battles for Chiang during the early stages of the Northern Expedition; and Mao Zedong, who in 1935 became the leader of the CCP.

Mao had been born a peasant, but ran away from home to study when he was a teenager. As a Communist, his major innovation was his **mobilisation** of the peasants as supporters and troops. Traditional Marxism had always focused on urban workers as the class that could lead a revolution, but Mao realised that the rural masses in China could fulfil the same role.

Mao was deeply convinced of the complete correctness of his views, and felt that only he understood what China really needed. He also believed that no revolution would be possible without violence. Even as the chief of a small rural base in the early 1930s, he had ordered the torture and killing of thousands of fellow Communists because they differed slightly from his own views.

The Sino-Japanese War

In July 1937, Japan launched an all-out assault on China, aiming for total conquest. This was the beginning of the eight-year **Sino-Japanese War**,

The Long March

In 1934, Nationalist troops were laying siege to the largest Chinese Communist base, which was located in the hills of Jiangxi province. On 16 October, around 80 000 Communists broke out under cover of darkness and fled to the west. Led by Mao Zedong, and pursued by Nationalist forces, they trekked for over 5000 kilometres until they at last settled in Shaanxi province in October 1935. The '**Long March**' quickly became a legendary example of Communist ingenuity and endurance – even though only a tiny fraction completed the trek.

Mao Zedong, leader of the CCP, addresses followers at Yenan during the Long March, 1937

which would eventually be merged with the Second World War. In the autumn of 1937 the Japanese took Shanghai after a colossal battle, and then moved up the Yangzi river to Nanjing, the Nationalist capital. Here, in December 1937, Japanese soldiers began a deliberate six-week outbreak of mass rape and murder, the so-called '**Rape of Nanjing**', in which it is estimated up to 300 000 people were killed. With Japanese forces advancing from the north and east, Chiang abandoned China's coastal provinces and withdrew far inland. For the rest of the war he would carry on fighting from the new capital of Chongqing.

Japanese soldiers celebrate the capture of Nanjing, China, in December 1937

By the end of 1941, the Nationalist resistance was on the point of collapse. But then the USA declared war on Japan following the Japanese attack on Pearl Harbor (see Unit 4, Chapter 4), and China became an ally of the United States. With US funding, supplies and military aid, the Nationalists could carry on their struggle for another four years. At last, when Japan surrendered to the USA in September 1945, all Japanese armies withdrew from China.

This was Mao Zedong's chance. During the war, the Communists had continued to win more and more support from the Chinese peasants, with CCP membership growing from 50 000 to 1.2 million. This was largely because their soldiers were strictly trained not to exploit local people by seizing food supplies or abusing women – a stark contrast with Nationalist troops, who regularly terrorised the peasants and seized supplies to fuel their war effort. By 1945 the GMD forces were exhausted from almost a decade of war, and had lost the backing of the Chinese masses. They had little hope of standing up to a Communist takeover.

Check your understanding

1. In what ways did the GMD government fail to reform China?
2. What were Mao Zedong's beliefs about the way to reform China?
3. Why is the Long March remembered as an inspiring event in Communist history?
4. How did the Japanese attack on Pearl Harbor save Chiang's regime from defeat?
5. Why were the Communists in a stronger position than the Nationalists by 1945?

Unit 6: Modern China
Mao's China

In 1946, the Chinese Civil War began. Under the command of Lin Biao, the **People's Liberation Army (PLA)** surged southward from the Communist bases in the north and north-east.

Control of the countryside meant that Communists could cut off rail and telegraph links, isolating the Nationalists in their urban strongholds. Soon, Nationalist armies began defecting to the Communists as city after city surrendered. Chiang and his surviving followers resisted stubbornly for three years, but in the autumn of 1949 they were forced to abandon mainland China and flee to the island of Taiwan.

The Communists were victorious. On 1 October 1949, in Beijing, Mao Zedong (now 'Chairman Mao') declared the formation of a new country: the **People's Republic of China**. Despite its name, the new 'republic' was a dictatorship, with all power concentrated in the hands of the CCP.

Taiwan

To this day, the Communist Chinese government claims that Taiwan is part of China, and officially expects that it will one day be re-integrated with the mainland. In practice, Taiwan has been a separate country ever since Chiang Kai-Shek fled there in 1949. Military rule by the GMD lasted for decades, continuing even after Chiang's death in 1975. Only in the 1980s did Taiwan become a democracy.

Transforming China

The Communists faced massive challenges. China remained overwhelmingly rural, and decades of warfare had left infrastructure wrecked and cities in ruins. Mao desperately needed international assistance. He got it from the Soviet Union, the world's established Communist superpower. Soviet dictator Josef Stalin sent experts to help modernise Chinese industry, and loaned China money to buy Soviet military equipment. With Soviet help, Mao began launching ambitious plans to transform China into a Communist society.

Business owners and 'bourgeois intellectuals', which in practice meant anybody who criticised the Party, were labelled as 'reactionaries' and 'enemies of the people'. Around 2.3 million of these people were imprisoned. Landowners in the countryside were massacred, with almost a million killed as their land was redistributed to the peasants. Peasants now owned their own farms, organised into 'mutual aid teams' for neighbouring families to work together.

Chinese cartoon circa 1950 showing Stalin and Mao Zedong's alliance weakening the West – the tiny figures to the left are US President Truman and British Prime Minister Winston Churchill.

In 1955, Mao went further and began the process of **collectivisation**. This meant that farms were combined into collective farms, with all land and tools under common ownership. This created much resentment from richer peasant families who were forced to give up their property to the collectives. By 1956 all villages had been collectivised, and all industry was state-controlled. Former factory owners and managers usually did not dare to speak out against the Party's takeover of their industrial property.

The final step came in 1957, when Mao began to combine the collectives into **communes**. Each commune contained between 20 000 and 100 000 people, and was designed to be a self-sufficient community in which all property and all work was shared between everyone. In these communes, life was often a significant improvement on the old rural life. The communes provided free services that had previously been rare or inaccessible, including childcare, healthcare, regular meals and schooling. Women living in the communes had much greater independence and equality with men than ever before in China. People had to put up with regular sessions of **indoctrination** in Communist ideology, and they were forced to give up their traditional ritual and religious practices. But many saw this as a small price to pay for a much more comfortable life.

A Chinese farmer kneels at gunpoint before a court enforcing land reforms in July 1952. He was later condemned and executed.

Tibet and the Dalai Lama

When the Chinese Empire collapsed in 1911, Tibet in effect became independent after centuries of semi-formal Chinese domination. Mao was determined to reverse this, and in 1949 China re-occupied Tibet. The 14th **Dalai Lama**, Tibet's religious and political leader, tolerated Chinese rule for 10 years. However, when Chinese troops crushed a Tibetan rebellion in 1959, he fled to India and established a **government-in-exile**.

The 14th Dalai Lama has come to be hugely respected internationally, as a Buddhist religious leader and a symbol of Tibetan freedom.

The 14th Dalai Lama, Tenzin Gyatso, circa 1960

Check your understanding

1. How did the Communists win the Chinese Civil War?
2. Why do the Chinese and Taiwanese governments disagree to this day about the status of Taiwan?
3. How did Mao Zedong reorganise communities in the Chinese countryside?
4. Why did the 14th Dalai Lama come to be so widely admired internationally?
5. How did ordinary life for Chinese peasants change under Mao's leadership up until 1958?

Unit 6: Modern China
Mao's famine

At the end of the 1950s, Mao's policies led to a catastrophic famine. This famine is sometimes said to have been the worst man-made disaster in the history of the world.

The Great Leap Forward

The roots of the famine lay in Mao's desire to drive up industrial production. It seemed that agricultural collectivisation had been a success: the 1957 harvest was spectacular, and under-production on China's farms looked like a thing of the past. Mao thought that just as the peasants had transformed agricultural production by working collectively, now they could do the same for industrial production.

At the same time, Mao was reacting against the new leadership in the USSR. Nikita Khrushchev, Stalin's successor, had recently rejected much of Stalin's legacy, declaring that Stalin had gone too far and caused needless suffering (see Unit 2, Chapter 5). Mao was outraged, and thought that the USSR was abandoning its commitment to revolutionary Communism. Even worse, some of the CCP's own leaders, led by Zhou Enlai, were soon proposing similar policies (see box). Mao feared that Khrushchev-style backsliding was taking hold in China. He grew determined that China would not slacken in its enthusiasm for revolutionary transformation.

The Hundred Flowers Campaign

In 1956, on the urging of Zhou Enlai, Mao suddenly announced that free expression and criticism of the Party would now be allowed. "Let a hundred flowers bloom!" he declared. However, after just a few weeks, Mao backtracked – and around half a million people who had expressed anti-Communist opinions were arrested.

Mao believed that by sheer force of will and revolutionary passion, China could be transformed in a handful of years into an advanced industrial nation. In the winter of 1957–8, he mobilised tens of millions of peasants to build dams, canals and reservoirs, creating a whole new water management infrastructure in a matter of months. Then, in January 1958, Mao officially announced a new campaign of economic development called the **Great Leap Forward**. The centrepiece of the Great Leap Forward was a plan to double China's production of steel from pig iron – not by building factories, but by using only the small **backyard furnaces** that already existed in Chinese villages.

A peasant tends a primitive backyard furnace during China's disastrous Great Leap Forward.

The road to famine

The Chinese people set to work, and began working day and night to smelt iron in their small furnaces. However, at the same time, they were also expected to keep up with the new levels of agricultural production. Producing both steel goods and a harvest soon proved impossible. The summer rains of 1958 caused many of the new dams and reservoirs built in the previous winter to collapse, flooding vast areas of farmland and destroying the crops. The desperate drive to keep the furnaces working around the clock meant that there was almost no fuel left over for cooking or heating. Usually the steel being produced was not even usable. Peasants soon began to die of malnutrition.

Desperate to meet their impossibly high production targets, and terrified of imprisonment or execution if they failed, commune officials reported grossly exaggerated levels of production – but it was all a lie. On paper, the 1959 harvest set a new record; in reality, food production had dropped by over 30 million tons. Communes were forced to hand over almost all the food they produced in order to meet the targets. Wheat was grown and sent off to the cities, while the people who grew it were left to eat grass and weeds. There was enough food in China to feed everybody, but sending grain back to the communes from the cities would have meant admitting that the Great Leap Forward had gone wrong. This was unacceptable: Mao believed that he had to be seen as **infallible**, meaning incapable of making mistakes. He therefore declared that any food shortages were the fault of bourgeois officials in the communes. Anybody who spoke out about what was happening was arrested as a reactionary. Doctors were even forbidden from putting 'starvation' as a cause of death on death certificates.

Food production on a commune during the Great Leap Forward

And so, famine swept the country, and peasants died in their millions. Minor diseases became fatal to people weakened by hunger, and to the old and very young. When children died, parents hid their bodies so that they would still receive their children's tiny ration of food. Soon the fields across China were lying fallow because there was nobody to sow the crops. Many people were driven to cannibalism in order to survive; often, they starved anyway.

Mao's great famine lasted for three years, from 1958 until 1961. It ended only because late in 1960, Mao finally relented and allowed other Communist officials to begin reversing his policies. We will never know exactly how many people died in Mao's famine, but it is estimated at between 30 and 40 million.

Check your understanding

1. Why were so many people arrested following the Hundred Flowers Campaign?
2. What did Mao plan to achieve with the Great Leap Forward?
3. Why were Chinese peasants unable to meet their steel production targets while also maintaining agricultural production?
4. Why did officials in the communes not give accurate reports of their production levels?
5. How did Mao's policies lead to the deaths of tens of millions of Chinese people from 1958 to 1961?

Unit 6: Modern China
The Cultural Revolution

After the famine, Mao stepped back from day-to-day government while a pair of officials named Liu Shaoqi and Deng Xiaoping took over the management of China.

Liu and Deng had a **pragmatic** approach to government and were not concerned with Communist purity. Deng famously remarked: "It doesn't matter if a cat is black or white, so long as it catches mice." The two of them downsized the communes, gave land back to individual families for private use, and allowed commerce in small markets. Productivity soon began to grow again.

However, Mao was plotting his comeback. He hated the new pragmatism, and was determined to restore an ideological direction to the CCP. Mao believed that revolutionary Communism could only stay alive through constant struggle and renewal – if things ever got too stable, society would become conservative and momentum would be lost. In order to shake China into turmoil, Mao planned to launch a radical new project: the **Great Proletarian Cultural Revolution**.

The Red Guards

In 1966, Lin Biao, Mao's closest ally, began organising Chinese students in the cities into groups called the **Red Guards**. These students had no memory of a time before Communist rule, and they were indoctrinated to follow Mao, no matter what. The students were told that China was full of reactionaries, and it was their job to root them out. In August, school and university classes were cancelled so that students could focus on the Cultural Revolution. They were soon putting up massive posters **denouncing** their parents, teachers and even Party officials as reactionaries. As Mao held massive rallies of Red Guards in Tiananmen Square in Beijing, groups of students began to attack and kill their teachers.

The aim was to destroy anything that remained of the pre-Communist past. Anyone with bourgeois habits, which could include keeping a pet or wearing foreign clothes, became a target. Over a billion copies of the **Little Red Book**, a collection of quotations from Mao, were printed and distributed across China to guide the Red Guards. By the spring of 1967, the Cultural Revolution had spread to the highest ranks of the Party, with tens of thousands of officials being expelled – including Liu Shaoqi and Deng Xiaoping. Deng's son was tortured and left

Red Guards reading Mao Zedong's Little Red Book at a rally in Beijing, China, 1966

permanently disabled, while Liu died after being denied medical treatment in prison. As the Red Guards continued to rampage, China seemed to be on the brink of anarchy.

In 1968, fearing that the forces he had unleashed were getting out of hand, Mao called upon the PLA to restore order. Lin Biao's army effectively took control of China. Millions of former Red Guards were now sent into the countryside to live as peasants – in theory, to spread the revolution among the common people, but in fact just to get them out of the cities.

Mao's last years

In April 1969, Mao designated Lin his official successor, and Lin seemed set to take over power from the now elderly and ailing chairman. However, on 13 September 1971, Lin fled Beijing on a plane with his wife. The plane crashed in Mongolia, and all on board were killed. Exactly what happened is controversial to this day. Mao claimed that Lin had been plotting to overthrow him, then tried to escape to the Soviet Union when his plot was uncovered. The incident shocked Mao's followers: how could Mao have misjudged somebody so close to him? Many began to lose faith in the Chairman's leadership.

China after Mao

In 1976, Mao Zedong died. His wife Jiang Qing was determined to carry on the Cultural Revolution, but she and her allies were quickly defeated and imprisoned. Most CCP officials wanted to move forward into an era of peace and stability. In 1978, Deng Xiaoping became the new Chinese leader. He believed that Mao's revolutionary leadership had failed China, and he intended to carry on with the pragmatic policies that he had attempted in the early 1960s.

Deng stayed in power through the 1980s, launching a process of reform and transformation that continues to this day. In the 21st century, China is a rich, industrialised and prosperous nation. The Communist Party still holds total political power, and China plays a major role in global politics. Mao Zedong is officially remembered as a great national leader who restored Chinese strength and independence, though the Party acknowledges that he made a number of errors later in his life. His embalmed body is kept in a mausoleum in Tiananmen Square, in Beijing.

The Nixon visit

In 1972, US President Richard Nixon visited China. After 23 years effectively cut off from the non-Communist world, the Communist leadership organised the visit in order to begin re-establishing Chinese global connections. Regular diplomacy and international trade soon followed.

US President Jimmy Carter and Deng Xiaoping pose outside the White House in Washington, DC, January 1979

Check your understanding

1. What policies did Liu Shaoqi and Deng Xiaoping pursue in the early 1960s?
2. What was Mao trying to achieve by launching the Cultural Revolution?
3. How did the Red Guards plunge China into chaos in the years 1966–8?
4. Why did the death of Lin Biao cause many of Mao's supporters to lose faith in him?
5. Why was most of the CCP leadership determined to change the way that China was governed after the death of Mao in 1976?

Unit 6: Modern China
Knowledge organiser

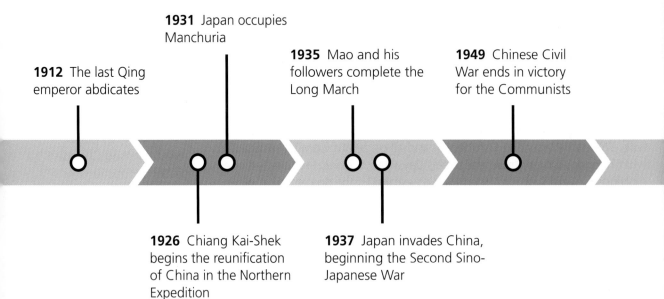

1931 Japan occupies Manchuria

1912 The last Qing emperor abdicates

1935 Mao and his followers complete the Long March

1949 Chinese Civil War ends in victory for the Communists

1926 Chiang Kai-Shek begins the reunification of China in the Northern Expedition

1937 Japan invades China, beginning the Second Sino-Japanese War

---

Key vocabulary

Autocrat A ruler who holds complete power, such as a dictator

Backyard furnaces Small, primitive coal-based ovens, used in Chinese villages for smelting pig iron into steel

Chinese Communist Party (CCP) Political party founded in 1921 and ruling China since 1949, based on Communist political theory

Collectivisation The process of combining privately owned farms into large 'collectives', which are farmed by groups of people under common ownership

Commune A mostly self-sufficient community, usually agricultural, in which all property and all work is shared

Cultural Revolution Officially the Great Proletarian Cultural Revolution, a campaign of radical violent transformation launched by Mao Zedong in 1966

Dalai Lama Tibetan Buddhist religious leader

Denounce Publicly condemn someone or something as bad or wrong

Guomindang (GMD) Chinese political party representing the Nationalist movement, led for many decades by Chiang Kai-Shek

Government-in-exile A national government that is based in another country because the country it leads has been occupied by a foreign power

Great Leap Forward Campaign of economic development, launched by Mao Zedong, which led to the great famine

Indoctrination The process of teaching somebody to accept a set of beliefs without questioning or thinking for themselves

Infallible Incapable of ever making mistakes

Long March Year-long trek by 80 000 Communists fleeing their Jiangxi base, remembered as a glorious event in the history of Communism

Little Red Book A book of quotations from Mao Zedong, distributed to Red Guards in the Cultural Revolution

Manchuria Large region in China's north-east, occupied by Japan during 1931–45

Mobilisation The process of organising large numbers of people for a purpose, often military or revolutionary

Nationalist Chinese political movement focused on Chinese strength and independence as a republic, identified with the Guomindang (GMD)

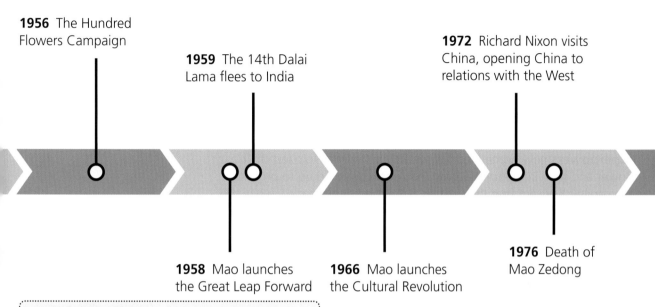

1956 The Hundred Flowers Campaign

1959 The 14th Dalai Lama flees to India

1972 Richard Nixon visits China, opening China to relations with the West

1958 Mao launches the Great Leap Forward

1966 Mao launches the Cultural Revolution

1976 Death of Mao Zedong

Key vocabulary

Northern Expedition Military campaign by Chiang Kai-Shek that reunited China and established Nationalist rule

People's Liberation Army (PLA) The army of the Chinese Communist Party and later of the People's Republic of China

People's Republic of China The official name of China since the Communist takeover in 1949

Pinyin The standard system for writing the Chinese language using the Latin (Western) alphabet rather than Chinese characters

Pragmatic Taking a realistic approach to something, based on doing what actually works instead of following beliefs or ideology

Rape of Nanjing Six-week outbreak of mass rape and murder committed by Japanese soldiers in Nanjing over the winter of 1937–8

Red Guards Groups of students formed in the Cultural Revolution to violently transform Chinese society

Sino-Japanese War War between China and Japan (can refer either to the 1894–5 war or to Chinese/Japanese conflict during the Second World War)

Warlords Independent military leaders who ruled over parts of China following the collapse of the Qing dynasty

Key people

Chiang Kai-Shek Nationalist leader who reunited China in the late 1920s and ruled for 20 years until losing the Chinese Civil War

Deng Xiaoping Pragmatic CCP official who began to reform China in the early 1960s and then became leader of the Party in 1978

Lin Biao Communist general who led the People's Liberation Army in the Chinese Civil War and later helped Mao to launch the Cultural Revolution

Mao Zedong Chairman of the CCP and People's Republic of China, who presided over the Communist transformation of China and disasters including the great famine

Sun Yat-Sen Original leader of the Nationalists and briefly president of China after the 1911 revolution

Zhou Enlai High-ranking Communist who wished to move the Party in a more moderate direction in the 1950s

Unit 7: The Cold War
Origins of the Cold War

For 45 years after the Second World War, the USA and the USSR confronted each other in a period of rivalry and tension called the Cold War.

Though they had worked together to defeat Nazi Germany, the Americans and the Soviets were deeply ideologically opposed. With the imperial powers of Europe effectively broken by the effort of war, the two **superpowers** now dominated the world – and aimed to exert their power and their influence globally. The Americans worked to protect the capitalist system that they shared with allied democracies, while the Soviets attempted to protect Communism and inspire other countries to adopt it. The USA and the USSR never actively went to war with each other in these years, but they worked against each other in every other possible way, through spying, diplomacy, economics and **proxy wars** (where the USA and USSR supported rival sides in wars involving smaller nations).

The Cold War in Europe

The Cold War split Europe down the middle. In 1944–5, Stalin's Red Army liberated almost the whole of Eastern Europe from Nazi domination. Those soldiers did not go home when the war was over. Instead, Stalin took the opportunity to impose Communist governments on the nations of Eastern Europe, including Poland, Hungary, Czechoslovakia, Bulgaria and Romania. Stalin's principal motive was to create a '**buffer zone**' of Soviet-friendly nations between the USSR and Germany, in order to guard against any future German attack.

Between 1945 and 1948, Communist parties in these countries, directed from Moscow, secured full political control. Sometimes there was a direct takeover, such as the coup in February 1948 that brought Communists to power in Czechoslovakia. More commonly, elections to form new governments were manipulated by violence, intimidation and fraud in order to produce Communist victories. Once control was secure, regimes were established that imitated the systems and techniques of Stalin's USSR. The newly Communist countries of eastern Europe were theoretically still independent nations, but in practice they became '**satellite states**' of the USSR – smaller, less powerful nations that depended on, and were directed by, the superpower. Eastern Europe had swapped one form of tyranny for another.

Alarmed by the spread of Soviet power, the US government resolved to do all it could to prevent Communism from spreading any further – a policy known as **containment**.

> ### NATO
>
> In 1949, the USA and the nations of Western Europe formed the **North Atlantic Treaty Organisation (NATO)**, a defensive military alliance that bound them all to defend each other against any external aggression.

Harry S. Truman (1884–1972)

In 1947, President Harry S. Truman declared that the United States would support any nation under threat from Communist revolution or attack. This was known as the **Truman Doctrine**, and it became the basis for US foreign policy throughout the Cold War.

Europe thus became divided into two spheres of influence under the two superpowers. In a speech in March 1946, when many observers already foresaw the complete division of Europe, Winston Churchill declared that "an iron curtain has descended across the continent". The term '**Iron Curtain**' soon became widely used to describe the division between capitalist American-allied Western Europe and Soviet-dominated Eastern Europe.

The Cold War in Asia

In Asia, the USA was focused on protecting its network of allied countries, and opposing the USSR and, from 1949, Communist China. The Americans nurtured pro-Western governments in Japan and Taiwan, and attempted to suppress Communist movements in Indochina and the Philippines.

Korea had been under Japanese occupation since 1910, but when Japan surrendered to the Allies in 1945, it was occupied by US forces in the south and Soviet forces in the north. Both superpowers withdrew in the late 1940s, but Korea was not reunited. Instead, two separate nations were established: democratic South Korea and Communist North Korea.

In 1950, North Korea attacked the south and the two nations went to war, with South Korea supported by the USA and North Korea by China. For almost three years, US and Chinese armies battled each other across Korea. Combat in the **Korean War** often resembled the static, trench-based warfare of the First World War, and neither side could secure a definite advantage. When an armistice was agreed in July 1953, the border between North and South Korea ran in roughly the same place that it had done in 1950. Approximately 3 million people had been killed, most of them Korean civilians. This was the first major proxy war of the Cold War.

Marshall Aid

One of the first consequences of the policy of containment was the **Marshall Plan**, a massive programme of financial aid that provided $12.7 billion of American money to help rebuild the nations of Western Europe. The US government feared that the postwar environment of poverty and ruin might cause the people of Western Europe to turn to Communism, in the same way that the Great Depression had led to the rise of the Nazis.

The Demilitarised Zone (no man's land) between North and South Korea

---

Check your understanding

1. How did Stalin impose Communist governments on the nations of Eastern Europe?

2. What was the Truman Doctrine?

3. Why did the United States provide Marshall Aid to the nations of Western Europe?

4. Why did the USA and China fight each other in the Korean War?

5. What were the causes of the Cold War?

Cold War Germany

The Iron Curtain ran right through the heart of the most strategically important nation in Europe: Germany. Throughout the Cold War, Germany was considered the 'front line' of the conflict.

In 1945, Germany was occupied by the USA, Britain and France in the west, and by the Soviet Union in the east. This division was never intended to be permanent, but it soon became clear that neither side was willing to give up control of their part of the country. Both sides feared that a reunited Germany would ally with the other against them, and so all negotiations on the subject eventually broke down.

Complicating this stand-off was the situation in Berlin. The German capital city lay deep within the Soviet zone. However, because of its political importance the city was divided just like the German nation: its western sectors were occupied by the USA, Britain and France, while the Soviet Union controlled the east. This meant that the western sectors of Berlin together formed a tiny pocket of Western control, over 100 kilometres behind the Iron Curtain.

The Berlin blockade

Truman and the leaders of Britain and France decided that if Germany was to remain divided, they would need to unite their three zones to form a single, independent West German nation. In June 1948, they introduced a new currency, the **Deutschmark**, in their zones of Germany – a clear signal that they intended to unite these zones to create a single country.

Stalin was furious. In response, he blockaded West Berlin, hoping to force the Western powers to give up their control of the city. Road and rail links between West Berlin and the world outside were suddenly blocked. Electricity was cut off, and all imports of food and fuel were halted. West Berlin in effect became an isolated island, under siege in the middle of Soviet-controlled territory.

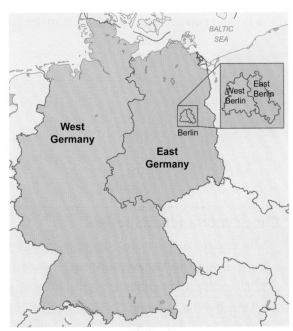

Map showing divided Germany and divided Berlin

The USA and Britain responded to the **Berlin blockade** by launching the Berlin airlift, a programme of supply that brought vital emergency rations to the city by airplane. Regular flights were soon ferrying thousands of tons of supplies to West Berlin every day. At the height of the operation, a plane was landing in Berlin every 90 seconds. This was vastly expensive at a time when Europe was still struggling to feed itself after the mass destruction of the war. Yet the Americans were determined to keep West Berlin alive and free from Soviet control. At last, when the airlift had been sustained through the winter, Stalin accepted that his attempt to intimidate the West had failed. The blockade was lifted in May 1949.

After the Berlin blockade, the Western zones of Germany were officially merged to create the new nation of **West Germany**, with its capital in Bonn. West Germany quickly became a stable, tolerant and peaceful country, widely regarded as a model of successful capitalist democracy. Under its first chancellor, Konrad Adenauer, it also boomed economically, surging ahead in prosperity to overtake the UK as the largest and most dynamic economy in Europe.

The Soviet zone, meanwhile, became **East Germany**. Like most of the other nations of Eastern Europe, East Germany was a Soviet satellite state. Its Communist leaders ruled over a country marked by poor living conditions and constant surveillance and censorship. A ruthless secret police agency called the **Stasi** directed a vast network of spies and informants to keep watch on the population, and anybody deemed to be disloyal to the regime was imprisoned, tortured or killed.

> ### Fact
> In East Germany there was one Stasi agent spying on every 166 citizens. This was a much higher level of surveillance than under the Nazi Gestapo, who had one spy for every 2000 citizens.

The Berlin Wall

Throughout the Cold War, West Berlin survived as a tiny, isolated outpost of West Germany: an island of freedom inside the Soviet empire. For some years it served as an escape route from Communism, as East German citizens who wished to flee their repressive government could come to Berlin, cross into the western sector and then take one of the trains that still connected West Berlin with the rest of West Germany. By the middle of 1961, almost 3 million people had fled from Communism by going through Berlin. However, the East German authorities could not allow this to continue.

In the early hours of 13 August 1961, the Communists built a wall around West Berlin, locking off the free city behind a concrete and barbed wire barrier. It was now almost impossible to cross from East Berlin into West Berlin without official permission. The escape route to the West was closed.

The **Berlin Wall** was seen to represent the failure of Communism. East Germany could not motivate its people to stay, so it had to stop them leaving by force. The wall also became an internationally recognised symbol of division, repression and tyranny.

The two sides of the Berlin Wall in 1962

Check your understanding
1. How were Germany and Berlin divided at the end of the Second World War?

2. Why did Stalin impose the Berlin blockade in June 1948?

3. How did the USA respond to the Berlin blockade?

4. Why did Communist East Germany build a wall around West Berlin on 13 August 1961?

5. Why is it sometimes said that Germany was the 'front line' of the Cold War?

Unit 7: The Cold War
Nuclear weapons

When the USA dropped atomic bombs on Hiroshima and Nagasaki in 1945, the world entered the nuclear age. The Cold War was defined by the possibility that these weapons might be used again.

The nuclear threat

The destructive power of nuclear weapons was (and remains) so great that the possibility of their use threatens the continued existence of human civilisation. Not only are nuclear explosions immensely large and destructive blasts, but they also release vast amounts of nuclear radiation, which damages living matter on a molecular level. Living things affected by radiation experience radiation sickness, which can lead to death within hours or even minutes. For those who are not exposed to enough radiation to die immediately, cancers swiftly develop. If for any reason large numbers of nuclear bombs were to be used, most living things on the planet would sicken and die.

Mushroom cloud of the atom bomb over Nagasaki

The USSR developed its own nuclear bomb in 1949. For the duration of the Cold War, the USA and the USSR both stockpiled nuclear weapons and were prepared at any moment to use them against each other. Both the Americans and the Soviets were relying on what is known as the **deterrent** effect. This is the theory that a nation possessing nuclear weapons will never have to use them, because nobody will dare attack it. When both the USA and the USSR were relying on their nuclear arsenals as deterrents, the effect worked both ways. If either of the superpowers used nuclear weapons against the other, the nuclear firepower unleashed by both would be so great that both nations would be wiped out – a situation known as **mutually assured destruction** (shortened to MAD). As a result, in theory, neither country would be willing to 'press the button'.

In practice, we now know that the world came close to near-total destruction several times during the Cold War, as both the Americans and the Soviets came within a whisker of deliberately or accidentally firing nuclear weapons. Probably the most dangerous of these near-misses, and the closest the world has ever come to nuclear war, was the Cuban Missile Crisis of 1962.

The Cuban Missile Crisis

In 1959, a Communist revolution led by Fidel Castro took place in the Caribbean island nation of Cuba. The Americans were alarmed by the presence of a Communist regime allied to the Soviet Union less than 150 kilometres from the US coastline. In 1961, the USA supported a failed attempt by CIA-trained Cuban exiles to overthrow Castro's government. This was called the **Bay of Pigs invasion**.

The leader of the Soviet Union at this time was Nikita Khrushchev, who came to power following the death of Stalin in 1953. In 1962, Khrushchev chose to station Soviet nuclear missiles in Cuba. This was to deter the USA from intervening again, and to provide nuclear protection for future Communist revolutions that Khrushchev hoped would take place in Central and South America. By sending missiles to Cuba, Khrushchev was actually placing the two superpowers

Fidel Castro and Nikita Khrushchev together

on a more equal footing, because the USA already had nuclear missiles stationed in Turkey at a comparable distance from the USSR. Nevertheless, when US spy planes detected the missiles in Cuba in October 1962, the news immediately triggered a crisis.

For 13 days the two superpowers were locked in a deadly stand-off. President John F. Kennedy imposed a naval blockade to prevent any more missiles from reaching Cuba, and demanded that Khrushchev dismantle and remove the missiles that were already there. Khrushchev refused to back down, and the world seemed to be on the brink of nuclear conflict. But at last, a deal was struck. Kennedy publicly pledged not to attempt any more invasions of Cuba, and in exchange Khrushchev agreed to withdraw the missiles. Secretly, Kennedy also agreed to remove the US missiles that were stationed in Turkey. The blockade of Cuba was lifted, and the world breathed a sigh of relief.

Recognising how close they had come to nuclear war, after 1962 both the USA and the USSR began making certain efforts to decrease tensions and to reduce the risk of conflict. In the later 1960s and 1970s the superpowers entered a period of **détente**, meaning slightly improved relations and limited but important cooperation. In 1972, a series of meetings called the Strategic Arms Limitations Talks led to a treaty called SALT I, which for the first time placed limits on the number of nuclear missiles that each side could possess.

Chernobyl

On 26 April 1986, there was an accidental explosion at the Soviet nuclear power plant at **Chernobyl**, in Ukraine. It released over a hundred times the radiation of the bombings of Hiroshima and Nagasaki combined. The atomic fallout was carried by the wind over much of Europe. Figures are disputed, but at least 4000 and perhaps closer to 100 000 people are estimated to have died from medical conditions directly linked to Chernobyl.

Check your understanding

1. What makes nuclear weapons so extraordinarily destructive?
2. What is the theory of the nuclear deterrent?
3. Why did Nikita Khrushchev station Soviet nuclear missiles in Cuba in 1962?
4. What agreement did Khrushchev and Kennedy make to resolve the Cuban Missile Crisis?
5. How did the superpowers attempt to limit the risk of nuclear war in the period following the Cuban Missile Crisis?

The Vietnam War

In Southeast Asia, the USA was drawn into arguably the most destructive conflict of the entire Cold War. This was the war in Vietnam.

Before the Second World War, imperial France ruled over **Indochina**, a colony encompassing the modern nations of Laos, Cambodia and Vietnam. French rule was swept away by Japanese conquest during the Second World War, and when Japan was defeated in 1945, the people of Indochina hoped to claim their independence. However, the French wanted their colony back.

The First Indochina War

The main independent political group in Vietnam was a communist party called the **Viet Minh**, led by a veteran Communist named Ho Chi Minh. During Japanese occupation, the Viet Minh had been supplied and funded by the United States as they fought against the invaders. Yet when Ho Chi Minh declared Vietnamese independence on the day of the Japanese surrender in 1945, the Americans were reluctant to support him. Fearing a Communist takeover, they instead supported the French attempt to regain control of Indochina.

The First Indochina War lasted from 1946 to 1954. During this war, the Viet Minh general Vo Nguyen Giap developed a guerrilla warfare strategy that would prove almost impossible to counter. Vietnamese communist soldiers learned to use the dense jungle to hide from the enemy, avoid open battle and instead mount surprise attacks on French army units. The French came to fear the next ambush and grew increasingly desperate as they struggled to even locate their enemy. When a large French garrison surrendered to Giap at Dien Bien Phu in May 1954, it signalled the end of the war. A peace agreement was signed at Geneva, and the French withdrew from Indochina.

Ho Chi Minh (1890–1969)

United States intervention

The agreement at Geneva was that Vietnam would be divided temporarily, with the north to be governed by the Viet Minh and the south to become an American-allied republic. Elections to reunite the country were scheduled for 1956. However, these elections were repeatedly delayed, because the USA feared that a reunited, Communist Vietnam would go on to spread Communism throughout Southeast Asia. As the Vietnamese grew steadily more frustrated with the slow pace of change, Ho Chi Minh eventually accepted that to achieve reunification and independence he would have to fight a second war, this time against the United States.

Communist guerrillas began attacking targets in the south in 1959, and the USA sent troops in response. US military commitments to Vietnam

Chemical warfare

The US military in Vietnam frequently used Agent Orange, a defoliant (chemical that makes trees shed their leaves) that also caused severe medical problems in those who were exposed to it. They also bombed villages using **napalm**, a highly flammable substance that clings to its targets while burning.

grew slowly through the early 1960s, with many troops officially labelled 'advisors' in order to disguise the reality that the country was entering a new war. However, in 1964 President Lyndon B. Johnson authorised a massive escalation, and it became clear that the USA was committed to the conflict. This was the Second Indochina War – more commonly known in the West as the Vietnam War.

Vietnamese Communist soldiers, known as the **Viet Cong**, were experts in jungle guerrilla warfare. The USA found themselves in the same position as the French, their vast military power rendered useless by an enemy they could not pin down. In addition, the Viet Cong wore no uniform, so it was impossible to tell which civilians in any Vietnamese village might in fact be

American helicopters dropping soldiers into the jungle during the Vietnam War

enemy soldiers, waiting to strike. Fearful and paranoid, the Americans resorted to launching 'search and destroy' raids: helicopter attacks on villages that very often led to massive civilian casualties. As the war dragged on, it became increasingly clear that the USA had no hope of victory, and was achieving nothing but mass violence.

The Vietnam War was the first war to be broadcast directly into people's homes via television. This caused much of the American public, shocked by what they saw, to abandon their support for the conflict. In 1973, President Richard Nixon withdrew US troops from Vietnam. Within two years, what remained of the American-allied South Vietnamese state had been overrun, with the Communists capturing the southern capital of Saigon in April 1975. Vietnam was reunited as a Communist nation. In the course of the war, 58 000 American soldiers had been killed. Estimates of Vietnamese casualties range from 1 million to almost 4 million military and civilian dead. It had taken almost 35 years of fighting, against Japan, France and finally the USA, for Vietnam to gain its independence.

The massacre at My Lai

In March 1968, several hundred unarmed Vietnamese civilians were killed in their village by an American army unit on a 'search and destroy' mission. The victims were mostly women, children and old men. Many of the women were raped before their deaths. The American army attempted to cover up the My Lai massacre, but it was exposed by journalists and caused shame and outrage back in the USA.

Check your understanding
1. Why did the USA support the French in the First Indochina War?
2. What was the strategy developed for the Vietnamese army by Vo Nguyen Giap?
3. Why did the Viet Minh launch a second war for Vietnam in 1959?
4. What were some of the reasons why so many Vietnamese civilians were killed by the Americans during the Vietnam War?
5. How did the Vietnam War come to an end in 1975?

The collapse of Communism

At the end of the 1980s, the USSR and its network of Eastern European satellite states rapidly collapsed, and Communism all but disappeared from Europe. The Cold War was over.

All this happened without the need for attack or sabotage by the West. Instead, the Soviet system failed on its own. For decades the USSR had been a stagnant society, with an economy that had stopped growing and was only a fraction of the size of the USA's. Few Soviet citizens believed in Communism anymore – they simply went through the motions and obeyed their leaders.

In 1985, Mikhail Gorbachev became the Soviet leader. Knowing that the country was failing, he hoped to revive it by launching reforms that would take the USSR in a new direction. Yet the process of change that he began would go further than Gorbachev ever intended, finally resulting in the abolition of the system he hoped to save.

Mikhail Gorbachev (born 1931)

The end of the USSR

Gorbachev had two major new policies: **glasnost** and **perestroika**. *Perestroika* ('restructuring') was an economic policy based on introducing elements of capitalism into the Communist system. The other policy, *glasnost* ('openness'), meant that Soviet citizens, including journalists, were now free to access government information, report and discuss it freely, and if they wished, criticise the government.

The effect of *glasnost* was explosive. Soviet media began attacking the government over everything from the apalling state of Soviet housing to the USSR's serious lack of environmental protections. Still hoping that public faith in the system could be restored, Gorbachev took the extraordinary step of allowing non-Communist candidates to stand in a nationwide election in 1989. The Communist Party still won the majority of seats, but it now faced open opposition.

Gorbachev was becoming increasingly unpopular with the Soviet people (even though he was admired in the West). This was because *perestroika* had led to food shortages and higher prices, making daily life worse for most ordinary people. In 1990, a prominent critic of Gorbachev named Boris Yeltsin was elected president of Russia. Yeltsin argued that Gorbachev's reforms did not go far enough, and called for a full transition to capitalism.

Some of the republics of the Soviet Union were seeking to become separate nations, with Lithuania declaring independence in March 1990. In August 1991, a small group of Communist Party politicians attempted to regain control of the USSR by launching a coup and placing Gorbachev under house arrest. They hoped to reverse Gorbachev's reforms.

The USSR and Russia

The Soviet Union was officially made up of 15 republics. Even though the term 'Soviet Russia' is often used to mean the whole USSR, Russia was technically only one of the republics within it.

Yeltsin spoke out against the coup and inspired massive protests against it, causing it to collapse. He then used his newfound authority to push for the complete separation of all remaining Soviet republics. On 26 December 1991, the Soviet Union was officially dissolved.

Democracy in Eastern Europe

While Communism was disintegrating in the USSR, pro-democracy movements campaigned for change in the satellite states. Gorbachev signalled in a speech at the United Nations in 1988 that he would not use the Red Army to enforce Communism in Eastern Europe. The people of the satellite states understood that they were free to go their own way. Many of their leaders, realising that Communism was failing, quietly made plans to give up power. In Poland, a free election was scheduled for June 1989.

Boris Yeltsin standing on a tank to address a crowd

The Polish election produced a government headed by **Solidarity**, a trade union turned political party. Solidarity had been formed in 1980, but because Communist governments were (in theory) meant to be run by the workers, the existence of an independent workers' union that opposed the government was an embarrassment. Solidarity had been banned and driven underground. Yet now they were in charge of Poland.

The election of Solidarity inspired the people of the other satellite states to reject their Communist rulers. Protesters poured onto the streets of Prague and Berlin. Hungary opened its border with democratic Austria, allowing residents of the Communist states to pass through Hungary and on into the West. On 9 November 1989, the East German Communists announced that they planned to allow free exit into West Berlin. Without waiting for confirmation, massive crowds of Germans in both halves of the city surged towards the Berlin Wall. The border guards laid down their weapons and abandoned their posts. Amid vast celebrations, the people of Berlin tore down the wall.

By the end of 1989, Communism had been overthrown in Poland, Hungary, East Germany, Czechoslovakia, Romania and Bulgaria. The transition was almost entirely peaceful: only in Romania did the Communists put up violent resistance to their removal, but they were swiftly defeated. In 1990, West and East Germany were officially reunited, becoming a single nation once again. Communism in Europe had disappeared into history.

The fall of the Berlin Wall in 1989

Check your understanding

1. What two new policies did Mikhail Gorbachev introduce in the Soviet Union?

2. Why did Gorbachev become so unpopular with the Soviet people?

3. Why was Boris Yeltsin able to push for the dissolution of the USSR in 1991?

4. Why did the Communist nations of Eastern Europe all abandon Communism in 1989?

5. How did the Berlin Wall come down?

Unit 7: The Cold War
Knowledge organiser

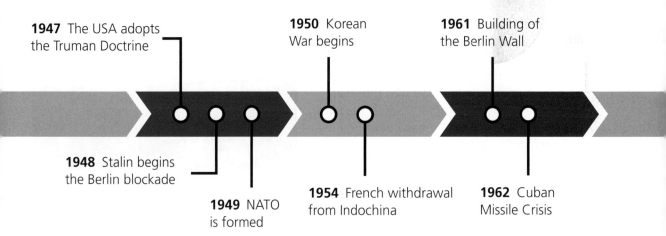

1947 The USA adopts the Truman Doctrine

1948 Stalin begins the Berlin blockade

1949 NATO is formed

1950 Korean War begins

1954 French withdrawal from Indochina

1961 Building of the Berlin Wall

1962 Cuban Missile Crisis

Key vocabulary

Bay of Pigs invasion Unsuccessful invasion of Cuba by US-backed Cuban exiles

Berlin blockade Attempt by Stalin to force the West to abandon West Berlin by blockading it

Berlin Wall Wall built by the East German Communists to physically separate West Berlin from East Berlin

Buffer zone Territory controlled or influenced by a nation, serving as a barrier to separate it from an enemy

Chernobyl Soviet nuclear power plant where there was a disastrous accidental explosion

Containment Policy of preventing Communism from spreading beyond the areas of the world where it was already established

Détente State of reduced tension and improved relations following a period of rivalry

Deterrent A weapon or threat that discourages people from doing something, even if it is never used

Deutschmark Currency introduced in the American, British and French zones of Germany, which sparked the Berlin blockade

East Germany Cold-War-era nation that was a satellite state of the USSR

Glasnost 'Openness'; Gorbachev's policy of allowing Soviet media and citizens to access government records and freely criticise the government

Indochina Former French colony in Southeast Asia that is now the nations of Cambodia, Laos and Vietnam

Iron Curtain The Cold War division between capitalist USA-allied Western Europe and communist Soviet-controlled Eastern Europe

Korean War Proxy war in which the USA supported South Korea and China supported North Korea

Marshall Plan Massive US financial aid programme that funded the reconstruction of Western Europe after the Second World War

Mutually assured destruction Situation in which two superpowers each possess enough nuclear weapons to destroy the other, so any war will result in the defeat of both

Napalm Chemical weapon used by the USA in Vietnam, that clings to its targets while burning

NATO North Atlantic Treaty Organisation, a military alliance of the USA with European nations for mutual defence

Perestroika 'Restructuring'; Gorbachev's policy of introducing elements of capitalism into the Communist economy by allowing small independent businesses to form

Proxy war War in which two powers fight each other indirectly by supporting rival sides in a war involving a smaller nation or nations

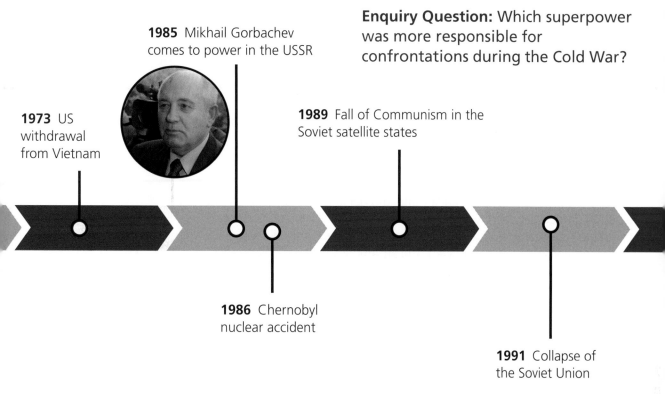

1985 Mikhail Gorbachev comes to power in the USSR

Enquiry Question: Which superpower was more responsible for confrontations during the Cold War?

1973 US withdrawal from Vietnam

1989 Fall of Communism in the Soviet satellite states

1986 Chernobyl nuclear accident

1991 Collapse of the Soviet Union

Key vocabulary

Satellite states Nations that are theoretically independent but in practice controlled by a superpower

Solidarity Polish workers' union that stood against the Communists as a political party, and formed the first government of post-Communist Poland

Stasi The secret police agency in Communist East Germany

Superpower Nation with the potential power to dominate the world

Truman Doctrine US foreign policy to contain Communism by intervening to support nations under threat

Viet Cong Term given to Communist guerrillas in South Vietnam during the Vietnam War

Viet Minh Communist party and independence movement in Vietnam

West Germany Cold-War-era nation allied with the USA

Key people

Mikhail Gorbachev Soviet leader who oversaw the collapse of Communism in Eastern Europe

John F. Kennedy President of the USA during the Cuban Missile Crisis

Nikita Khrushchev Soviet leader who stationed nuclear missiles in Cuba, beginning the Cuban Missile Crisis

Ho Chi Minh Leader of the Vietnamese Communists during both Indochina Wars

Harry S. Truman President of the USA during the beginning of the Cold War, who established the policy of containment

Boris Yeltsin Russian politician and rival to Gorbachev who pushed for the dissolution of the USSR and then became the first president of post-Soviet Russia

The American Civil War

In the United States of America, the abolition of slavery was not achieved peacefully. Instead, the struggle grew into a massive civil war that threatened to tear the new republic apart.

When the United States of America came into being in 1776, it was already a nation divided between two societies. In the Southern states, slavery was central to American life. Around one in four families were slave-owners, and plantations worked by enslaved African Americans (growing cotton, sugar and tobacco) were essential to the economy. In the Northern states, far fewer people were enslaved, and slavery was gradually abolished during the early 19th century. White Southerners fought bitterly against any attempt by the Northern states to limit their rights as slave-owners.

Harriet Tubman

Harriet Tubman was a former enslaved African American who escaped her captivity and made it to the North in 1849. She then ran a series of missions into the South to rescue those who were enslaved and guide them to freedom, relying on a secret network of abolitionists and safe houses called the **Underground Railroad**. During the 1850s, Tubman successfully freed dozens of enslaved African Americans.

Harriet Tubman (1820–1913)

"A house divided"

Southerners argued that enslaved African Americans were actually better treated than the White working class in the North, and that poor White Southerners were able to live in greater dignity because the worst work was done by those who were enslaved. They also argued that Black people were unable to look after themselves, and therefore that freeing them would be cruel and irresponsible.

Although few Northerners supported abolition throughout the USA, some of them were growing uneasy with the spread of slavery and feared the growing power of Southern senators in Congress. In 1854, a new political party was founded called the **Republicans**, based entirely in the Northern states and dedicated to fighting the 'slave power'. The tension between abolitionists and slave-owners was becoming explosive.

Abraham Lincoln (1809–65)

In the election of 1860, the Republican candidate, Abraham Lincoln, was elected president. During his campaign, Lincoln emphasised the message that America could not survive as a nation half slave-owning and half free. He famously repeated the Biblical warning: "A house divided against itself cannot stand." For Southerners, Lincoln's election was the final straw. Refusing to be governed by him, in December 1860, South Carolina **seceded** from the Union, officially declaring itself no longer part of the United States. The rest of the South soon followed – 11 states in total. They formed a breakaway nation, the **Confederate States of America**, with a man named Jefferson Davis as their president. Lincoln and the North were determined not to allow it. They resolved to fight to preserve the Union.

Civil war

In the war that followed, the North won because of its higher population (more than double that of the South) and its vast industrial power. The might of US industry, four-fifths of it located in Northern states, was mobilised to produce huge quantities of armaments and machinery. The primarily agricultural South was blockaded from overseas trade, and by 1864, its economy was broken and its population starving.

Lincoln had gone to war to preserve the Union, not to end slavery. However, as the war went on, events overtook him. Enslaved African Americans in the South were refusing to obey orders now that their masters were away fighting, and Northern opinion was growing more radical. The great abolitionist Frederick Douglass, himself a former enslaved person, declared: "Fire must be met with water, darkness with light, and war for the destruction of liberty must be met with war for the destruction of slavery." In 1863, Lincoln issued the **Emancipation Proclamation**, which ended slavery and made all enslaved people in the South free.

On 9 April 1865, the veteran Southern general Robert E. Lee, commander of the Confederate army, surrendered to the Union in a small Virginian village named Appomattox. After four years of warfare and over 600 000 dead, the United States were reunited. Five days later, Abraham Lincoln was at the theatre when a Southern fanatic named John Wilkes Booth shot and killed him. Lincoln became a martyr for the cause of emancipation and has been honoured by Americans ever since.

The Gettysburg Address

The decisive clash of the American Civil War was the Battle of Gettysburg, fought over several days in July 1863. An estimated 50 000 soldiers were killed or wounded, and it took months to clear the corpses from the battlefield. When a cemetery was finally opened on 19 November, Lincoln attended and gave a short speech. The **Gettysburg Address** became one of the most famous speeches in US history. Lincoln stated that the North was fighting to preserve the true values of the American republic. He promised "that these dead shall not have died in vain, that this nation under God shall have a new birth of freedom, and that government of the people, by the people, for the people, shall not perish from the earth."

Check your understanding

1. How did Harriet Tubman attempt to liberate others from slavery?
2. What did the Southern states do in response to the election of Abraham Lincoln in 1860?
3. Why did the North win the American Civil War?
4. What was Lincoln's message in the Gettysburg Address?
5. How did the American Civil War bring about the end of slavery in the United States?

Unit 8: Civil Rights in the USA
Segregation and terror

With slavery abolished, many White Americans sought new ways to deny the Black population any real freedom. In the South, they built a social system designed to create a permanent Black underclass.

The Jim Crow South

In 1860, there were approximately 4 million enslaved African Americans in the United States out of a total population of around 31 million. When the civil war was over, they had their freedom, but they were trapped in a society that was determined to deny them equal rights. The Southern states passed laws that became known as the '**Jim Crow**' **laws**, requiring Black Americans to live their lives almost entirely separately from White Americans. This was the system known as **segregation**, meaning the enforced separation of races. It was a legal injustice that would endure for a hundred years.

A segregated waiting area at the Public Health Service Dispensary in Washington, DC.

In the Jim Crow South, Black Americans were forced to attend separate schools, live in separate housing, eat in separate restaurants and even use separate toilets. Black people were required to use separate entrances for public buildings and to sit in separate sections (at the back) on public transport. In theory, all facilities were meant to be 'separate but equal', but in practice this was almost never enforced. Schools for Black people were underfunded; housing districts were crowded and poorly built; toilets were squalid. Any Black person who attempted to enter a Whites-only venue or use facilities for White people would be arrested, probably imprisoned, and very often beaten up by police or White bystanders.

Segregation was upheld by the **Supreme Court** – America's highest legal authority, which holds the power to interpret and enforce American law. When Homer Plessy deliberately sat in a Whites-only part of a train in order to test the legal system, the resulting Supreme Court case, *Plessy v. Ferguson* (1896), ruled that segregation was wholly legal. There was nothing Black Americans could legally do to overturn the oppressive regime under which they were forced to live.

Who was Jim Crow?

Jim Crow was a character created by a minstrel show actor around 1830. The name became widely used as a derogatory term for Black Americans.

Prison labour

The Thirteenth Amendment to the US constitution, which abolished slavery, stated: "Neither slavery nor involuntary servitude, except as punishment for a crime whereof the party shall have been duly convicted, shall exist within the United States." The inclusion of the clause on criminal punishment created a loophole, meaning that Black people could still be enslaved for hard labour if they were convicted of a crime. Huge numbers of Black men were arrested on trumped-up charges and in effect re-enslaved as prisoners. Groups of labouring prisoners called 'chain gangs' became a common sight in the South.

Lynching and terror

In the Jim Crow South, the inferior position of Black people was routinely enforced by violence. Black people who did not show the expected level of respect towards White people were **lynched**, meaning murdered by a White mob. Lynchings were common and usually went unpunished.

One organisation in particular made it their goal to terrorise Black communities. In 1866, Confederate ex-soldiers in Tennessee founded the **Ku Klux Klan** (from the Greek *kuklos*, meaning 'circle'). The Klan's mission was to enforce White supremacy in America. Wearing white robes and pointed white hoods, and carrying burning crosses, the Klan took the lead in lynching Black people across the South. The possibility of Black men having sex with White women was a particular obsession, and countless Black men were lynched following accusations of rape or of making sexual advances. The Klan also targeted Republican voters and used intimidation to enforce support for the **Democrats**, who were traditionally the party of the South. By the 1920s, the Klan had between 2 and 5 million members from all across the USA – one in six, they claimed, of the eligible White population.

Nocturnal gathering of the Ku Klux Klan, 1921

Fleeing segregation and White violence, Black people migrated from the South in vast numbers. In what became known as the 'Great Migration', well over a million left during the 1910s and 1920s, followed by another surge during the Second World War. The large Black populations that exist to this day in major Northern cities, such as Chicago, New York and Philadelphia, were founded by these migrants. However, Black communities in the North still faced discrimination, forced to live in crowded ghettoes and usually working in only the most menial jobs. After all, despite the differences in their history, many Northerners were every bit as racist as their Southern counterparts.

Emmett Till

In August 1955, Black 14-year-old Emmett Till was visiting relatives in rural Mississippi. One day he walked into a grocery store staffed by White 21-year-old Carolyn Bryant. After Emmett left the store, Carolyn told her husband he had flirted with her. Several nights later, her husband and two other men abducted Emmett from his relatives' house, beat him, killed him and dumped his body in a river. Emmett Till's lynching became a national media story, yet the incident was not very different from the thousands of lynchings that regularly took place in the South. In 2008, in her old age, Carolyn Bryant admitted that she had made up the accusations.

Emmett Till (1941–55)

Check your understanding

1. How did the Jim Crow laws create a segregated society in the American South?
2. How was the prison system used to re-enslave Black men?
3. What did the Ku Klux Klan do to enforce White supremacy?
4. Why was Emmett Till murdered in August 1955?
5. Why did so many Black Americans migrate out of the South between the civil war and the 1950s?

The Civil Rights Movement

In the 1950s and 1960s, a massive movement by Black Americans fought for equal rights. This was the Civil Rights Movement.

Challenging segregation

The National Association for the Advancement of Colored People (NAACP), which was the USA's leading civil rights group, opened the way by launching a targeted legal challenge to segregation in schools. This led to a Supreme Court case called **Brown v. Board of Education** (1954). Black lawyer Thurgood Marshall successfully argued that separate educational facilities were unavoidably unequal by their very nature, and therefore unconstitutional. The court agreed. However, the judges chose not to demand immediate desegregation, but left it up to state governments – which were controlled by White Americans – to implement the decision at their own pace. The result was that no action was taken.

Rosa Parks sat in a 'Whites only' section of a public bus in Montgomery, Alabama. This photo was taken at some point after the boycott.

The Montgomery bus boycott

The event that is usually seen as the beginning of the Civil Rights Movement (along with Emmett Till's murder) happened on 1 December 1955 in Montgomery, Alabama. Rosa Parks, an experienced Black civil rights activist, sat in the 'Whites only' part of a bus and refused to give up her seat to a White man. She was arrested. On the day of her trial four days later, the Black community in Montgomery started a boycott of all the city buses. The city was filled with Black men and women solemnly walking to work, sharing car rides, or if they could not find a way to travel, staying at home and risking their jobs.

At a meeting that same evening, representatives of the local Black community formally founded an organisation to fight for social justice. As their leader, they elected a 26-year-old Christian minister named Martin Luther King Jr. With a PhD in theology and great talent as a preacher, King's leadership was characterised by firm moral resolve, inspiring rhetoric and a determined insistence on non-violence. Even when his house was bombed several months into the bus boycott, King always preached forgiveness. As he would declare in 1961: "Ours is a way out – creative, moral and non-violent. It is not tied to Black supremacy or communism but to the plight of the oppressed. It can save the soul of America."

Martin Luther King Jr (1929–68)

The **Montgomery bus boycott** was King's, and the Black community's, first major success. It lasted for almost a year, until in November 1956 the Supreme Court ruled that segregation on the city's buses was unconstitutional. By now, Martin Luther King was becoming a nationally recognised figure.

The Little Rock schools crisis

In 1957, some schools in the South were finally being desegregated following local campaigns. In the town of Little Rock, Arkansas, nine Black students were enrolled in the formerly all-White Little Rock Central High School. When the school year began, however, Arkansas governor Orval Faubus chose to block school **integration** by sending in the Arkansas National Guard (the state-controlled military force). The soldiers were ordered to prevent the Black students from entering the school.

Dwight D. Eisenhower, Republican President of the USA from 1953 to 1961, had been reluctant to push for change in the South. He believed that social change must happen naturally in its own time, and that forcing it only leads to chaos and social breakdown. However, Eisenhower could not allow a state government to directly defy a Supreme Court order. He nationalised the Arkansas National Guard (placing it under the control of America's **federal government** in Washington, DC) and then sent the federal army into Little Rock with orders to protect and escort the Black students into the school. Despite constant racial harassment from their White peers, the students stuck out the school year. However, in the following year, Faubus shut down all Little Rock's public schools rather than accept more Black students. It took another Supreme Court order to force the schools to reopen.

Civil disobedience

In 1960–1, there was a wave of **civil disobedience** across the South. The most common tactic was to stage **sit-ins**: Black students trained in non-violent protest techniques, often directly inspired by Gandhi's leadership in India (see Unit 9, Chapter 1), would sit at a Whites-only lunch counter in a department store and refuse to move when they were not served. When police arrested them, another wave of students would sit down in their place – and so it went on, no matter how many were arrested. Black men were regularly beaten in prison by White police and guards, but the Civil Rights Movement was turning the act of getting arrested into an act of protest.

Black American musicians

Most of the USA's distinctive forms of music were invented by Black people. Jazz evolved in the 1920s among Black musicians in New Orleans, and was popularised by artists such as Louis Armstrong. Rock'n'roll, the style that forms the basis of all modern rock and pop music, was pioneered in the 1950s by Black musicians including Chuck Berry and Little Richard. Because they were Black, however, they could not become big commercial stars. It was Elvis Presley, a White singer performing rock'n'roll in the style of these Black songwriters, who became America's biggest musical celebrity of the 20th century. Elvis played the key role in popularising the new music around the world.

Chuck Berry (1926–2017)

Check your understanding

1. What was the result of the Supreme Court case *Brown v. Board of Education*?
2. How did Rosa Parks trigger the first major protest of the Civil Rights Movement in December 1955?
3. What kind of leadership did Martin Luther King Jr provide for the Civil Rights Movement?
4. Why was there a crisis over school integration in Little Rock, Arkansas, in 1957?
5. What did President Eisenhower do in response to the Little Rock crisis?

The victories of the 1960s

The Civil Rights Movement reached its climax in the early years of the 1960s, when Martin Luther King and his fellow campaigners succeeded in overthrowing the Jim Crow laws.

From Birmingham to Washington

In 1963, Martin Luther King targeted Birmingham, Alabama, for marches and sit-ins. This was the South's most segregated city and a stronghold of the Ku Klux Klan. King understood that protesting in Birmingham would provoke a violent crackdown, and he chose to lead the movement there because he wished to challenge and expose White supremacy in its most open and undeniable form. King was arrested at a march and imprisoned, but the protests succeeded once again in focusing attention on the Civil Rights Movement.

The Birmingham campaign was such a success that King chose to keep the momentum going by leading a march to Washington itself. On 28 August 1963, King stood on the steps of the Lincoln Memorial and addressed a crowd estimated at a quarter of a million people. He made what is perhaps the most famous speech in all of history: his "I have a dream" speech. "Now is the time to make real the promises of democracy," he declared. "I have a dream that one day down in Alabama, with its vicious racists, … one day right there in Alabama little Black boys and Black girls will be able to join hands with little White boys and White girls as sisters and brothers. I have a dream today."

Police remove demonstrators outside City Hall in Birmingham, Alabama

That day in Washington is often seen as the high point of the Civil Rights Movement. Bowing to public pressure, President John F. Kennedy prepared a civil rights bill for Congress. Before he could implement it, he was killed – shot by an assassin in Dallas, Texas, on 22 November 1963. But his vice president Lyndon B. Johnson, who now replaced Kennedy, carried the bill forward. On 2 July 1964, the **Civil Rights Act** was passed. It made all forms of segregation and discrimination illegal, in every part of the United States.

King's letter from Birmingham City Jail

During his imprisonment, King wrote what became one of the defining statements of his politics, the **Letter from Birmingham City Jail**. In it, he explained how non-violent protest was designed to force White Americans to negotiate: "It seeks so to dramatise the issue that it can no longer be ignored." He went on, "My friends, I must say to you that we have not made a single gain in civil rights without determined legal and nonviolent pressure. History is the long and tragic story of the fact that privileged groups seldom give up their privileges voluntarily. … We know through painful experience that freedom is never voluntarily given by the oppressor; it must be demanded by the oppressed."

Martin Luther King in Jefferson County Jail in Birmingham, Alabama

The Voting Rights Act

Across the South there remained one other massive legal barrier to racial equality: restrictions on Black people's access to voting. It was deliberately made extremely difficult to **register to vote**. Registrar offices were open for only a few days a month, for short periods, so that Black Americans were forced to risk their jobs by taking time off work to go through the registration process. This process itself involved highly complex tests, sometimes requiring applicants to know the names of obscure government figures such as the attorney general, or to explain complex congressional procedures. The names of newly registered voters would also be published in local newspapers, exposing them to violence in retaliation.

In 1965, King led a march in Selma, Alabama, to protest against voting restrictions. King, many local teachers who joined the march, and hundreds of their students were all arrested. When King next attempted to lead a long march from Selma to the state capital, Montgomery, local police (many of them on horseback) blocked the bridge out of Selma. When the marchers refused to turn back, the police charged at them, fired tear gas at the crowd and beat up dozens of protesters.

The police violence shocked the nation. President Johnson, responding in outrage, rushed to pass the **Voting Rights Act** in August that year. This law forced states to eliminate barriers to Black registration. In Mississippi alone, the proportion of eligible Black voters who were registered jumped from under 10 per cent in the early 1960s to over 60 per cent by 1968. This was immensely empowering: when large numbers of Black Americans could vote, they could begin electing their own representatives to fight for them.

Martin Luther King at the march on Washington, 1963

The view of over 200 000 marchers along the Capitol at the march on Washington

Check your understanding

1. Why did Martin Luther King choose Birmingham, Alabama, as the target for one of his major protests?
2. What points did King make in his *Letter from Birmingham City Jail*?
3. How did President John F. Kennedy respond to the march on Washington of 28 August 1963?
4. How were Black Americans prevented from registering to vote in most of the South?
5. What was the result of the protests in Selma, Alabama, in 1965?

Unit 8: Civil Rights in the USA
Unfinished struggle

American society had been permanently reshaped, but equality under the law did not automatically mean equality in practice. Racism endured, and the fight for justice was far from over.

A radicalised nation

As the 1960s wore on, the mood in the United States turned bitter. The Civil Rights Movement did inspire other disadvantaged groups to launch or renew their own struggles for equality, with feminist organisations, Native American groups, and the gay rights movement all making demands for social justice. However, the visibility and success of Black rights activism had provoked an angry racist backlash. In every summer during the mid-1960s, there were violent clashes in cities across the USA, most of them sparked by incidents of White police brutality. The most serious were the **Watts riots** in Los Angeles in 1965, which lasted for six days and saw looting and burning across nearly 130 square kilometres of the city. Many conservative Americans felt that the society they knew was disintegrating around them.

Focusing all the various strands of protest was the USA's war in Vietnam (see Unit 7, Chapter 4), which became the dominant political issue of the era. Vietnam created a division in American society between those who supported the war and those who opposed it. Anti-war feeling was strongest among young people and Black Americans. In the late 1960s, vast crowds of protesters joined peace marches in cities across the USA.

For younger Black Americans, the racism that they still faced on a daily basis caused many to feel that even greater radical change was needed. In both North and South, Black people were still systematically discriminated against in jobs and housing. They were denied employment and promotion opportunities, and were sold and rented inferior houses at higher prices. When King turned his attention to these issues, he found that the movement's tried-and-tested tactics did not work in Northern cities, where there was no formal segregation and thus no obvious targets for civil disobedience. A march in Chicago in 1966 to protest against housing inequality produced minimal results.

Black Power

In the mid-1960s, the **Black Power** movement emerged. This was a form of protest that emphasised racial pride, accepted a need for the use of force in Black self-defence, and called for Black control of resources in Black communities. The Black Power protesters worried many White Americans, who feared a slide into violence. When two Black US athletes at the 1968 Olympics gave the Black Power salute (a raised fist) in front of a global audience at the medal ceremony (see next page), they were condemned by most White Americans and suspended from the US team.

Malcolm X

Malcolm X was a radical civil rights leader who believed that King's non-violent strategy was holding Black Americans back. The 'X' in his name symbolised the lost African name taken from his ancestors by slavery. Malcolm X believed that Black Americans needed to rise up to create their own society, by force if necessary, and to encourage unity with other Black people across the globe. He was assassinated in 1965, but his ideas influenced the Black Power movement and he remains a symbol of Black pride.

Malcolm X (1925–1965)

In fact, Black Power protesters never actually resorted to violence, even though they threatened it. The same could not be said of the **Black Panthers**, a militant Black liberation group founded in San Francisco in 1966. The Black Panthers combined traditional civil rights activism with Marxism and opposition to American imperialism (as they saw it, the global use of United States military and economic power to exploit other nations). They believed in self-defence by violence when necessary, and were involved in frequent clashes with the police. The Black Panthers attracted the attention of the FBI, and they were eliminated by the end of the 1960s.

As American politics grew harsher, Martin Luther King began to voice more radical views. King feared that the Civil Rights Movement had ultimately only benefited middle-class Black people, and began to suggest that the American system itself was unjustly and cruelly slanted against the poor of all races. However, King would never have the chance to develop these ideas. On 4 April 1968, as he was standing on a hotel balcony in Memphis, Tennessee, an assassin shot and killed him.

King's murder shocked and traumatised the USA. It was widely felt that the assassination symbolised all the many disappointments and failures of the later 1960s. Segregation had been legally dismantled, but little had changed in most Black people's experience. In some parts of the United States, segregation remains very severe, and the work of the Civil Rights Movement continues to this day.

American runners giving the Black Power salute during the Olympic Games, 1968

Nixon's Southern strategy

At the 1968 election, there was a major shift in the political landscape of the United States. White Southerners had traditionally voted Democrat, but now a pair of Democratic presidents, Kennedy and Johnson, had thrown their support behind Black civil rights. Richard Nixon, the Republican candidate in 1968, realised that he could win huge numbers of votes by appealing to White Southerners who were disappointed with the Democrats. This '**Southern strategy**' won Nixon the election. From this point onwards, the Republicans would rely on the White South for their core support, while the Democrats became more associated with civil rights causes. The two parties had essentially swapped positions.

Check your understanding

1. Why was there an increase in social tension in the United States in the late 1960s?
2. What made the ideas of Malcolm X different from established civil rights activism?
3. Why was there a scandal when two US athletes gave the Black Power salute at the 1968 Olympics?
4. How did the voting habits of White Southerners change during the 1960s?
5. How were Martin Luther King's political ideas beginning to change in the period before his death?

Knowledge organiser

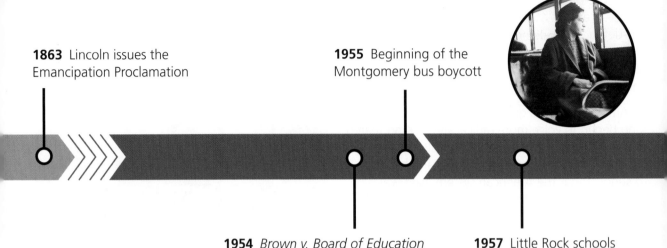

1863 Lincoln issues the Emancipation Proclamation

1955 Beginning of the Montgomery bus boycott

1954 *Brown v. Board of Education*

1957 Little Rock schools integration crisis

Key vocabulary

Black Panthers Militant group that aimed to use force to win more rights for Black Americans

Black Power Movement that broke away from the established Civil Rights Movement to emphasise Black pride and reject integration

Brown v. Board of Education US Supreme Court case that ruled that segregation in schools was unconstitutional

Civil disobedience Protest tactic based on the non-violent refusal to obey laws that are considered unjust

Civil Rights Act Law that made all forms of segregation and discrimination illegal in the USA

Confederacy (Confederate States of America); breakaway nation formed by the Southern states of the USA during the American Civil War

Democrats In the USA, political party traditionally representing the White South, later becoming the USA's major progressive party

Emancipation Proclamation Decree by Abraham Lincoln ending slavery in the USA

Federal government Government of the whole United States, based in Washington, DC, separate from the governments of individual states

Gettysburg Address Speech given by Abraham Lincoln when dedicating the cemetery after the Battle of Gettysburg

Integration Process of different groups of people learning to live or work together in a functioning and positive way

Jim Crow laws Laws in Southern states enforcing segregation between White and Black Americans

Ku Klux Klan (KKK) White supremacist organisation dedicated to enforcing the dominance of White Americans through violence

Letter from Birmingham City Jail Document written by Martin Luther King Jr outlining his political philosophy

Lynching Murder of a Black person by a White mob

Montgomery bus boycott Campaign targeting segregation on city buses in Montgomery, Alabama

Registration to vote Process of enrolment that confirms a citizen's right to vote in elections, and which is required before they can do so

Enquiry Question: "The success of the Civil Rights Movement was due to the leadership of Martin Luther King." To what extent do you agree?

1961 Civil disobedience campaign by the Freedom Riders

1964 The Civil Rights Act

1965 (August) The Voting Rights Act

1968 (November) Republican Richard Nixon is elected US President

1963 Martin Luther King Jr's march on Washington

1965 (March) Protest marches in Selma, Alabama

1968 (April) Assassination of Martin Luther King Jr

Republicans In the USA, political party formed to oppose the Southern states where slavery continued, later becoming the nation's major conservative party

Secede Withdraw from a nation or union to become independent

Segregation Forced separation of different ethnic groups in most aspects of life

Sit-ins Civil disobedience tactic in which Black people would deliberately sit at a Whites-only lunch counter or other segregated area

Southern strategy Electoral strategy of appealing to White Southerners, pioneered by Richard Nixon and adopted by most Republican presidents after him

Supreme Court Highest court of the USA, possessing enormous power to shape United States law

Underground Railroad Secret network of abolitionists who helped enslaved African Americans who had escaped captivity in the South before the civil war

Voting Rights Act Law that required all states to remove barriers to Black Americans registering to vote

Watts riots Massive race-based riots in Los Angeles in 1965

Key people

Lyndon B. Johnson Democrat President who passed the Civil Rights Act and Voting Rights Act

Martin Luther King Jr Main leader of the Civil Rights Movement, who emphasised non-violent protest

Abraham Lincoln President who governed the North during the American Civil War and issued the Emancipation Proclamation

Thurgood Marshall Black American lawyer who won the *Brown v. Board of Education* case; later the first Black judge to sit on the Supreme Court

Richard Nixon President who replaced Lyndon B. Johnson and won support for the Republicans by appealing to White Southerners

Rosa Parks Black activist whose refusal to give up her seat on a city bus began the Montgomery bus boycott

Emmett Till Black teenager lynched in 1955, whose murder became a nationwide scandal

Malcolm X Radical civil rights leader who believed that Black Americans needed to create their own independent society, using force if necessary

Unit 9: Decolonisation
Decolonising Ireland

During the 20th century, most of the European colonial empires fell apart, including the British Empire. For Britain, decolonisation began with its oldest colony, Ireland.

As the century dawned, Ireland was still formally part of the UK. For decades, Liberal governments had sought to introduce Home Rule for Ireland: the restoration of a parliament to Dublin, and self-government within the UK. Home Rule was the short-term goal of the Irish **Republican** movement, which represented the rural Catholic majority and ultimately aimed for full independence. However, in **Ulster** in the north of Ireland, there was a large Protestant community descended from English and Scottish settlers. These were mostly **Unionists**, meaning they wanted Ireland to remain part of the United Kingdom and be governed from London. The Unionists threatened violent uprising if Home Rule were ever introduced.

The partition of Ireland

In 1914, the British government at last passed a bill establishing Home Rule, but then delayed its implementation until the end of the war. Yet before the war could finish, one group of Republicans launched a direct attempt to wrest control from the British. On Easter Monday in 1916, around 1600 protesters led by Patrick Pearse and James Connolly took control of several public buildings in Dublin, making their headquarters in the central Post Office. They declared Ireland a republic and proclaimed themselves a provisional government. Over four days of fighting, British soldiers violently suppressed the **Easter Rising**, and its leaders were executed.

The brutality of the British response alienated huge numbers of Irish and fuelled support for full independence. In the British election of December 1918, every Irish constituency outside Ulster elected candidates from **Sinn Féin**, the leading Republican political group. Refusing to take their seats in London, the Sinn Féin candidates instead convened their own parliament in Dublin, the Dáil Éireann. In 1919, the Dáil once again declared Ireland a republic – and the Irish War of Independence erupted. Resistance to British rule was now organised by the **Irish Republican Army (IRA)**, the military wing of Sinn Féin.

The war ended in December 1921, when Michael Collins, commander of the IRA, signed the Anglo-Irish Treaty. When it came into force the next year, this made most of Ireland independent but kept six of the nine counties of Ulster within the UK. They became Northern Ireland. The new independent Irish nation immediately entered a 10-month civil war, fought between those who supported the treaty and those Republicans who wished to continue fighting for Ulster. However, the Republicans eventually chose to accept the partition (division) of Ireland. The island has remained divided ever since.

Lady Constance Markiewicz

One of the Sinn Féin candidates elected in 1918 was Lady Constance Markiewicz, the first woman to be elected to the UK Parliament (though she did not take her seat).

The Black and Tans

The '**Black and Tans**' (so called because of their mixture of police and army uniforms) were a group of British men recruited to reinforce the British police force in Ireland. They were mostly former soldiers who had come straight from the Western Front and were responsible for terrible violence in Ireland, including mass rape, torture, massacres and burning down homes.

The Troubles in Northern Ireland

Northern Ireland, the newest country of the UK, was very hostile to the Catholic Irish minority in its midst. Catholics faced widespread discrimination and were shut out of key professions, including the civil service, judiciary and police. From the late 1960s to the 1990s, there was renewed violence in Northern Ireland – a period known as the '**Troubles**'.

The Troubles started when Catholic civil rights protesters in 1969 were confronted by Protestant 'loyalist' counter-protesters. The resulting violence prompted the British government to send in the army to keep the peace, but this in turn provoked further conflict. Violence between Unionist militants, Republican militants and the British Army escalated. The most notorious incident occurred in January 1972 when British paratroopers in Londonderry (Derry) killed 13 civilians, an event known as Bloody Sunday. By the time the Troubles were over, 3600 people had been killed, and one in five Ulster residents had a family member killed or wounded in the fighting.

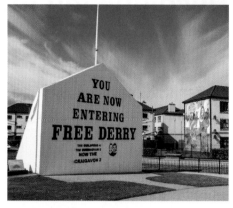

Catholic mural in Londonderry (Derry), Northern Ireland

The key Republican paramilitary group was a new version of the Irish Republican Army, the Provisional IRA (named after the provisional government declared during the Easter Rising). This new IRA pursued a 30-year campaign of bombings and shootings both in Ireland and on the British mainland. Their goal was to make Northern Ireland ungovernable through violence. On the opposing side, the largest Protestant militant group was the Ulster Defence Association (UDA), which, like the Provisional IRA, committed frequent terrorist attacks throughout the three decades of the Troubles.

Protestant mural in Belfast, Northern Ireland

In 1997, Tony Blair's Labour government opened direct negotiations with Sinn Féin under its leader Gerry Adams. The result was the **Good Friday Agreement** of 1998, which brought an end to the Troubles. The agreement formally established the rights of the Irish nationalist minority in Northern Ireland – including guaranteed representation in a new local parliament, the Northern Ireland Assembly. It also removed border checks and instituted permanent close cooperation between the Irish and Northern Irish governments, finally restoring normal life for Irish people in both countries.

Assassination attempts

The Provisional IRA made at least two attempts to assassinate a British prime minister. In 1984, Margaret Thatcher narrowly escaped being killed by a bomb in Brighton. In 1991, mortar shells were fired into 10 Downing Street while John Major was having a cabinet meeting.

Check your understanding

1. What is the difference between the Republican and Unionist movements in Ireland?

2. What were the consequences in Ireland of the British election of December 1918?

3. How did the Anglo-Irish Treaty resolve the conflict in Ireland?

4. How did the Provisional IRA attempt to end British rule in Northern Ireland?

5. Why did the Troubles come to an end in 1998?

Decolonising the Middle East

British imperial rule in the Middle East had existed for a much shorter period than in Ireland, and yet it would leave an even more complex and troubled legacy behind it.

Britain and the Arabs

During the First World War, the British supported the Arab Revolt against the Ottoman Empire (see Unit 1, Chapter 4). They promised the leader of the Arabs, Sharif Hussein, that they would support the creation of an independent Arab state when Ottoman rule of the Middle East was overthrown. But secretly, the British had already made plans to keep the Ottoman territories for themselves. In May 1916, before the Arab Revolt even began, the diplomats Sir Mark Sykes of Britain and François Georges-Picot of France made a secret agreement to divide the Middle East between their two empires. France was to get what became Syria, and Britain was to get what became Iraq and Jordan. This was called the **Sykes–Picot Agreement**.

The Arab army during the Arab Revolt of 1916

When the Ottomans surrendered in 1918, the Arab inhabitants of the Middle East were ignored by the European powers. Through the League of Nations, a new organisation intended to resolve international conflicts, Britain and France were given mandates to rule Iraq, Jordan and Syria. This meant that the European powers were in charge of running these countries until they judged that the local people could be trusted to take over for themselves. In practice, it was simply a new form of European colonial rule.

In these new British and French colonies, the outraged Arabs demanded to be given real control of their lands. Armed rebellion became common, and both Britain and France struggled to hold their new imperial possessions together.

The troubles in Palestine

Among the promises made by the British to Hussein and his allies was that the Arabs of Palestine, the coastal region containing Jerusalem, would have their independence. Palestine, however, was also the focus of a nationalist ideological movement among some sectors of the Jewish community. This was **Zionism**, the movement to establish a nation state for Jewish people in their ancient homeland. In 1917, the British officially declared their support for Zionism in a statement known as the **Balfour Declaration**. In effect, the British had now promised the same piece of land to two different groups of people.

After the First World War, Britain took over the administration of Palestine through another League of Nations mandate. At this time there were around 600 000 Arabs living in Palestine and around 80 000 Jews. Jewish immigration, however, was swiftly growing, and soon there were frequent anti-Jewish riots by the Arabs. The situation grew worse after the Nazis took power in Germany, as Jewish refugees from Europe headed to Palestine in the hope of safety. In 1937, a British government report concluded that the claims of the two sides were incompatible. By the 1940s, there was constant guerrilla warfare in Palestine between Jewish and Arab militant groups.

British withdrawal

Recognising the reality of Arab nationalism, the British granted partial independence to Jordan in 1928 and to Iraq in 1932. However, in the Second World War both grants of independence were revoked. The Allies considered it vital to protect their supply of oil from the Middle East in order to keep their planes and ships running, and so both Iraq and Jordan were reoccupied. Only after the war did the British finally withdraw fully from the region, as did the French from Syria. All three countries would face troubled futures, due in part to the artificiality of the borders and institutions forced on them by Europeans.

Because of the Holocaust and with the emergence of a strongly pro-Zionist policy in the United States, there was widespread international support after the Second World War for the creation of a Jewish state in Palestine. On 14 May 1948, the nation of Israel was officially proclaimed. It was immediately attacked by Egypt, Jordan and Iraq, expressing the outrage of much of the Arab world. Israel won this war, but the future appeared uncertain. A massive 750 000 Palestinian Arab refugees were soon living in camps in Jordan and Egypt. The displacement of these Palestinians bred a huge amount of mistrust and hatred towards the new state of Israel. Recurring violence between Arabs and Israelis has continued to the present day.

> ### Saudi Arabia
>
> In the Arabian peninsula to the south of Iraq, a long-running struggle for power between Hussein and a rival Arab king, Abdulaziz (called 'Ibn Saud' by Westerners), ended in victory for Abdulaziz in 1932. Abdulaziz and his family, the **House of Saud**, established the new kingdom of Saudi Arabia. The kingdom would grow immensely rich, thanks to newly discovered reserves of oil. This wealth would make it one of the most powerful of the new Arab countries.

Displaced Palestinian Arabs during the 1948 exodus (known in Arabic as the Nakba, meaning 'catastrophe')

Check your understanding

1. How was the Middle East reorganised by League of Nations mandates after the First World War?
2. Why were there competing claims for control of Palestine from the First World War onwards?
3. Why did the new kingdom of Saudi Arabia quickly become one of the most powerful Arab countries?
4. Why did the British reoccupy Jordan and Iraq during the Second World War?
5. Why was Israel attacked by a coalition of Arab nations immediately upon its creation in 1948?

Unit 9: Decolonisation
Decolonising India

In India, an independence movement had existed since the 19th century. However, it was only when Britain was severely weakened by the Second World War that India finally won its independence.

At the beginning of the 20th century, the British **Raj** was being undermined from within by a steadily growing nationalist movement. This movement was based in the Indian National Congress (often called the **Congress Party**), a predominantly Hindu political group founded in 1885. Though it still pledged 'unswerving loyalty' to the British crown, the British authorities viewed the Congress Party as a threat and refused to cooperate with it.

During the First World War, Prime Minister David Lloyd George drew up plans to introduce complete self-government for India gradually, while keeping it within the Empire. However, in 1919 the British administration in India not only failed to honour these promises of self-government, but passed a law called the Rowlatt Act that allowed Indian activists to be arrested and imprisoned indefinitely without trial. Riots broke out in response. At Amritsar, on 13 April, Colonel Reginald Dyer ordered his troops to fire on an unarmed crowd. At least 400 Indians, perhaps over 1000, were killed. The **Amritsar massacre** remains one of the most notorious atrocities in the history of British colonial rule.

Indian independence

After Amritsar, Indian nationalism became more focused, as many Indians concluded that the British would only give up control of India when forced to. The man who now emerged as leader of the independence movement was a Hindu lawyer and activist named Mohandas Gandhi. He was known by the honorary title Mahatma, meaning 'Great Soul'. Gandhi led a campaign of civil disobedience, which included strikes, boycotts of British courts and schools, refusal to serve in British government jobs, refusal to pay taxes, sitting and blocking streets, and hunger strikes in prison. Gandhi's non-violent strategy became an inspiration to independence movements across the world. For many Indians, he came to be viewed almost as a holy man.

Despite Gandhi's leadership, by 1930 a major religious division had appeared within the nationalist movement. Hindu and Muslim activists increasingly disagreed about what form the future nation should take. Gandhi's leadership and prestige helped to hold the nationalist movement together, smoothing over divisions between Hindus and Muslims. However, this did not stop some Muslim activists from arguing that when independence was won, there should be a separate nation for Muslims created in India's north-west.

Ruling India

India was Britain's largest and most important colony. Indian tax revenue provided the British Empire with a vital income, while Indian troops were key to its defence. George Curzon, British **viceroy** of India at the dawn of the 20th century, once declared: "As long as we rule India, we are the greatest power in the world. If we lose it, we shall drop straightaway to a third-rate power."

Mahatma Gandhi (1869–1948)

When Japanese armies advanced across Asia in 1942, the Congress Party called upon Britain for immediate independence by passing the 'Quit India' resolution. In response, the British arrested tens of thousands of Congress leaders, including Gandhi, and banned the Party. Protests erupted across India, and over 100 000 people were imprisoned. The British ruled India under martial law for the remainder of the war. In the process, they oversaw a devastating famine in Bengal in 1943, in which around three million Indians died. The British occupation policy involved printing money to pay for wartime costs, driving up prices uncontrollably and so causing the famine. Churchill also refused to send food that could have alleviated the famine, insisting that it should all be reserved for feeding soldiers who were fighting the war.

When Clement Attlee's government came to power in 1945, it offered full independence to India and declared that it would hand over control no later than June 1948. This extremely short timetable prompted both Hindu and Muslim nationalists to push for the **partition** (division) of India into separate nations, having no time to negotiate a compromise that might have held them together. As a result, on 15 August 1947, two new nations came into being: India, a secular but majority Hindu nation; and Pakistan, an Islamic republic.

Immediately there were massive population transfers, as many Hindus and Muslims migrated between the two countries to ensure they lived in safety and under a government of their own religion. The British official Cyril Radcliffe had been given only five weeks to draw the border between India and Pakistan, so in many places it did not reflect real divisions between local communities. In areas where minorities were left stranded, tens of thousands of people were massacred. Gandhi was assassinated in January 1948 by a Hindu extremist for attempting to halt the violence. Animosity between India and Pakistan has endured to the present day.

People migrating to their chosen nation during the Indian partition

Check your understanding

1. What plan did David Lloyd George form in response to Indian nationalism?
2. Why were 400 Indians massacred at Amritsar on 13 April 1919?
3. How did Mahatma Gandhi use civil disobedience to campaign for Indian independence?
4. How did Britain respond to the 'Quit India' resolution in 1942?
5. Why did the creation of India and Pakistan lead to mass violence in both nations?

Unit 9: Decolonisation
The Suez Crisis

In 1956, Britain attempted to use armed force to regain control of a key part of its empire. The result was failure and humiliation.

The rise of Nasser

In 1922, Britain had granted partial independence to Egypt, but kept control of the Suez Canal. The canal remained vital for Britain to keep control of its global empire, because of the access it provided to India and Middle Eastern oil. For Egyptian nationalists, the continuing presence of British soldiers in the canal zone was felt to be an insult.

In 1952, a group of strongly anti-British army officers took power in a revolution. One of them, Gamal Abdel Nasser, soon became President of Egypt. He was an inspirational leader who soon came to be regarded as a global hero of anti-colonialism. A committed Egyptian nationalist, Nasser wanted the British to leave Egypt for good.

Gamal Abdel Nasser (1918–70)

Nasser had grand plans to modernise Egypt, and the centrepiece of these plans was to be a new hydroelectric dam on the Nile at a place called Aswan. The **Aswan High Dam** would allow Egypt to massively increase food production by better controlling the flooding of the Nile, and it would provide electricity for millions of Egyptians. The British and Americans had offered to finance the construction of the dam, pledging a loan of $270 million. However, in 1956 this offer was withdrawn. Nasser had recently signed an arms deal with Communist Czechoslovakia, and Britain and the USA wanted to show Nasser that they would not support him if he grew closer to their Communist enemies.

Nasser responded in a way that nobody had expected. In July 1956, he **nationalised** the Suez Canal, placing it under the direct control of the Egyptian government. Nasser argued that Egypt needed an alternative source of revenue to pay for the Aswan High Dam, and the profits from the control of the canal would fund the dam within five years.

Britain's response

Outrage erupted in Britain. The canal was widely seen as a vital possession in Britain's shrinking empire, and much of the public was affronted at the thought of losing it. Prime Minister Anthony Eden went even further: he saw Nasser as a new Hitler, who would launch a similar career of aggression if he was not stopped. Eden began making secret plans with France and Israel to regain control of the Suez Canal and remove Nasser from power.

In October 1956, Israel invaded the canal zone. This was done in order to give Britain and France

Port Said after the attack of British and French troops

an excuse to intervene. Claiming that free movement through the canal was in danger, the two former imperial powers launched an airborne and seaborne invasion to 'protect' the canal. To observers worldwide, it was obvious that Britain, France and Israel had manufactured a crisis in order to take back the canal. All three countries publicly denied this, but very few people were fooled.

The Algerian War

There was a reason why France was happy to collude with Britain to remove Nasser from power. Nasser was an outspoken supporter of the independence movement in Algeria, a French colony, where an uprising against French rule had begun in 1954. The Algerian War lasted until 1962, and involved a series of brutal crackdowns by the French army against the guerrilla resistance movement and Algerian civilians. In the end, France was forced to accept Algerian independence.

Foolishly, Anthony Eden had assumed that the United States would support the invasion of the canal zone. He had not even informed them of the plan in advance. To Eden's shock, US President Dwight D. Eisenhower was furious with all three aggressors. Eisenhower opposed European imperialism, and he feared that British and French meddling in the Arab world would encourage Arab countries to side with the USSR in the Cold War. He therefore demanded that Britain, France and Israel all withdraw from Egypt. In order to enforce this demand, Eisenhower threatened to block a much-needed loan to Britain from the International Monetary Fund (IMF). Britain was still rebuilding its economy after the Second World War, and the loss of this money would have caused a massive financial crash. Eden was forced to call off the invasion, and the French and Israelis had no choice but to withdraw their forces as well. Eisenhower commented in private, "I've just never seen great powers make such a complete mess and botch of things."

Nasser emerged from the Suez Crisis triumphant: the Egyptian people saw him as a hero for standing up to the British. For Britain, the Suez Crisis was a national humiliation. It clearly demonstrated the loss of British status and power on the world stage, and that the USA now held much greater power to decide international affairs. The Suez Crisis is often seen as the definitive endpoint in the history of the British Empire as a global power.

Check your understanding
1. Why did Britain and the USA withdraw their offer to finance the construction of the Aswan High Dam in 1956?
2. What plan did Britain, France and Israel form in response to the nationalisation of the Suez Canal?
3. Why was France willing to go along with Britain's efforts to remove Nasser from power?
4. How did Dwight D. Eisenhower force Britain to abandon the invasion of the canal zone?
5. What were the consequences of the Suez Crisis for Nasser and for Britain?

Decolonising Africa

The British Empire in Africa consisted of well over 20 colonies covering huge areas of the continent. By the mid-1960s, almost all were independent.

In colonial Africa, the borders between the many European colonies were often little more than lines drawn on a map. The 19th-century 'Scramble for Africa' had created a patchwork of imperial territories that bore little relation to the real African communities on the ground. Ethnic and linguistic groups were split apart and lumped together with no regard for their own identities or interests. This meant that when the European powers withdrew, many of the new African nations faced futures of division, civil conflict, and the oppression or persecution of minorities.

African independence movements

In 1957, Ghana (formerly the Gold Coast) became the first of Britain's sub-Saharan African colonies to become independent. This came after almost a decade of strikes and protests led by the man who now became president, Kwame Nkrumah. He was at the forefront of a wave of independence movements driven in part by **Pan-Africanism**, which meant solidarity between all African nations and the liberation of all territories still under Western rule. After Ghana, other British colonies quickly followed: Nigeria became independent in 1960, Uganda in 1962, Kenya in 1963, and Malawi and Zambia in 1964.

For Kenya, independence came only after a decade of violence. In 1952, a group officially called the Land and Freedom Army, usually known as the Mau Mau, launched a violent uprising against British rule in Kenya. It mostly represented the Kikuyu people, one of Kenya's main ethnic groups. The British suppressed the **Mau Mau revolt** not only by fighting the militants, but by detaining hundreds of thousands of Kenyan people in concentration camps. Prisoners in these camps died from disease, torture and forced labour. Though figures are disputed, the British are thought to have killed some 50 000 Kenyans during the revolt. A state of emergency lasted until 1960.

In the following decades, the British government denied that human rights abuses had been committed during the Mau Mau revolt, and therefore the revolt became a deeply controversial issue. Only in 2013 did a court case force the British government to pay £20 million in compensation to survivors of the concentration camps.

South Africa

In the so-called settler colonies – those governed by populations of White immigrants – independence came by a very different route. Cape Colony became a self-governing dominion under the name

The Commonwealth of Nations

Founded in 1931, the **Commonwealth** is a global association of 54 nations with strong links to the UK. Almost all of them are former colonies of the British Empire, but all share equal status within the organisation. The Commonwealth is perhaps best known today for the Commonwealth Games, a sporting competition hosted every four years by one of the Commonwealth nations.

A British soldier examines the papers of an African cyclist at gunpoint in the search for Mau Mau insurgents, Nairobi, Kenya, 1953

South Africa in 1910. Here, a White (Dutch and British) minority held power over a much larger Black African majority. In 1948, the National Party came to power in an election. This was a party dedicated to enforcing White supremacy over the Black population. Its core supporters were the **Afrikaners**, the descendants of Dutch settlers (formerly known as the Boers), but it also had broad support among all White South Africans.

The National Party constructed a system of racial segregation called **Apartheid**. Apartheid began in 1950 with the Population Registration Act, a law that classified all inhabitants of South Africa as White, Black, or mixed race. More laws soon followed that used this classification system to regulate where South Africans could live, what schools they could attend, what jobs they could work in, and which public facilities they could use. Black South Africans were barred from voting, restricted to inferior schools and jobs, and kept apart from White South Africans. A series of Land Acts even set aside more than 80 per cent of the country's land for the White minority. Violence aginst Black South Africans was common. The aim of Apartheid was to permanently guarantee White supremacy in South Africa.

The entrance to the Apartheid Museum in Cape Town shows an example of the segregation signs seen in the country during Apartheid.

In 1961, South Africa declared full independence from Britain and became a republic, after fears grew that Britain would try to force South Africa to grant more rights to its Black population. Apartheid lasted until the early 1990s, when the constitution was re-written and Black South Africans won full equal rights. This happened only after decades of international pressure and determined struggle by Black South Africans. One of the leaders in the anti-Apartheid movement, Nelson Mandela, became the country's first Black president after spending 27 years in prison. He won a landslide victory in the national election of 1994.

Zimbabwe

In 1965, Southern Rhodesia declared independence from Britain. Conditions here were similar to South Africa: a small minority of White settlers dominated a much larger Black population, and they hoped that independence would allow them to construct a system similar to Apartheid. However, eventually the White government was forced to agree to equal voting rights for all. The country was renamed Zimbabwe in 1980.

Check your understanding
1. Why did many African nations experience serious civil conflict after gaining independence from their European colonisers?
2. What was the first sub-Saharan African colony to become independent from Britain?
3. How did the British suppress the Mau Mau revolt in Kenya during the 1950s?
4. How did Apartheid separate White and Black South Africans?
5. Why did South Africa declare itself a republic in 1961?

Unit 9: Decolonisation
Knowledge organiser

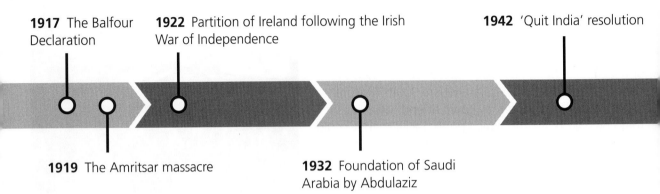

1917 The Balfour Declaration

1922 Partition of Ireland following the Irish War of Independence

1942 'Quit India' resolution

1919 The Amritsar massacre

1932 Foundation of Saudi Arabia by Abdulaziz

Key vocabulary

Afrikaners White inhabitants of South Africa who were descended from Dutch settlers

Amritsar massacre Atrocity in which at least 400 Indian protesters were killed when British soldiers fired on the crowd

Apartheid Policy of racial segregation in South Africa that enforced White supremacy for most of the second half of the 20th century

Aswan High Dam Massive hydroelectric dam on the River Nile

Balfour Declaration British government statement establishing official support for Zionism

Black and Tans British paramilitary troops that fought in the Irish War of Independence, known for their brutality

Commonwealth of Nations Global association of 54 nations with strong links to the UK, mostly former British colonies

Congress Party Indian National Congress, a Hindu-dominated political party that spearheaded the independence movement

Easter Rising Rebellion against British rule in Ireland in 1916

Good Friday Agreement Agreement between the British government, Irish government and Northern Irish parties, which ended the Troubles

House of Saud Royal family that founded Saudi Arabia and continues to govern it

Irish Republican Army (IRA) Military wing of Sinn Féin, which fought for Irish independence and later (as the Provisional IRA) fought on one side in the Troubles

Mau Mau revolt Uprising against British rule in Kenya

Nationalise Place an industry or company under direct government control

Pan-Africanism 'All-Africanism'; belief in solidarity between African nations against colonial powers, or in the unification of African nations

Partition The division of a region into two or more separate territories or nations

Quit India Resolution passed by the Congress Party in 1942 demanding the British immediately withdraw from India

Raj Term for British-ruled India from 1858 until Indian independence in 1947

Republicans In Ireland, those who supported Irish independence; later, those who wished to reunite Northern Ireland with Ireland

Sinn Féin The leading Republican political party in Northern Ireland

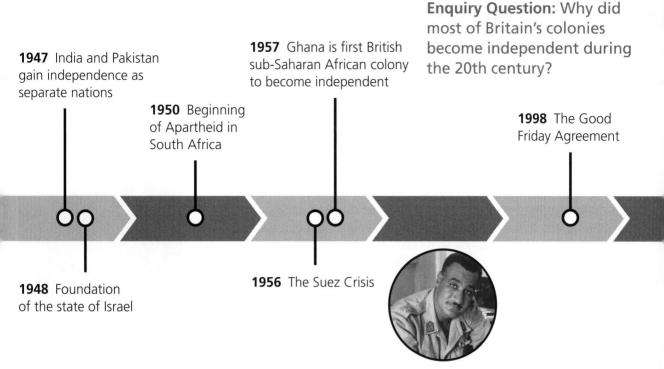

1947 India and Pakistan gain independence as separate nations

1950 Beginning of Apartheid in South Africa

1957 Ghana is first British sub-Saharan African colony to become independent

Enquiry Question: Why did most of Britain's colonies become independent during the 20th century?

1998 The Good Friday Agreement

1948 Foundation of the state of Israel

1956 The Suez Crisis

Key vocabulary

Sykes–Picot Agreement Secret diplomatic agreement between Britain and France in 1916 to divide the Middle East between them after the defeat of the Ottoman Empire

Troubles Thirty-year period of violence between Republican and Unionist groups in Northern Ireland

Ulster The northern region of Ireland, part of which remained in the United Kingdom in 1922 and became Northern Ireland

Unionists In Ireland, those who support remaining part of the United Kingdom

Viceroy Official in charge of ruling British India

Zionism The movement to establish (later to maintain) a nation state for Jewish people in the region that is now Israel

Key people

Abdulaziz Founder of Saudi Arabia, often known in the West as Ibn Saud

Michael Collins Commander of the IRA during the Irish War of Independence

Anthony Eden British prime minister during the Suez Crisis

Mohandas Gandhi Prominent leader of the Indian independence movement, who advocated non-violence and civil disobedience

Nelson Mandela Anti-Apartheid campaigner who then become the first Black president of South Africa

Gamal Abdel Nasser Nationalist president of Egypt during the Suez Crisis

Kwame Nkrumah First president of independent Ghana and a leader of the Pan-African movement

The welfare state

The scale of injury, death and destruction during the Second World War led to an increasing realisation that only the government had the amount of power needed to rebuild the country.

In 1942, the economist William Beveridge published a report advocating for social reform in Britain. Within a year it had sold over half a million copies – an unprecedented number for a government report. Although the Second World War had helped to erode some class boundaries, Britain remained a very hierarchical society. Beveridge identified 'five giants' that were causing large disparities between the rich and the poor, and he offered solutions for how the state could help to solve these issues (see box below).

In return for a weekly contribution, an individual would have the right to receive financial benefits when in need throughout their lifetime. These contributions were a joint commitment by individuals and the state to provide cover against the risks of sickness, injury, unemployment and poverty. This new form of 'social security' would provide protection 'from cradle to grave'. It would apply to the whole nation, would be universal instead of selective, and children would also be covered.

William Beveridge, the influential postwar economist, in 1947

The 'five giants'

Beveridge identified "five giants on the road to postwar reconstruction" that needed to be addressed to ensure Britain enjoyed a stable and prosperous future, along with solutions for how to remove them:

- WANT – National Insurance for anyone unemployed or unable to work; a family allowance system for those with children
- DISEASE – a National Health Service for free access to GPs and treatment in hospitals
- IGNORANCE – raising the school leaving age to 15; expanding on the number of universities and scholarships
- SQUALOR – a vast house building programme to clear Victorian slums and replace homes destroyed by bombing
- IDLENESS – guaranteed employment for those able and willing to work.

Labour Party victory

The Labour Party was founded in 1900 to promote **socialist** ideas and try to give a voice to the working classes. Labour leader Clement Attlee served as the Deputy Prime Minister during Churchill's wartime coalition government. As the Second World War neared its end, a **general election** was called for 5 July 1945. The Labour Party **manifesto**, 'Let Us Face the Future', set out a bold vision to transform British society, incorporating the ideas presented in the Beveridge Report. They promised that if they won the election, they would create a government that would take responsibility to care for all its citizens, regardless of their background or wealth.

When the results came in it was clear the Labour Party had won a landslide victory, with 146 more seats in the House of Commons than any other party, and were able to form the first Labour majority government. Churchill was shocked that his Conservative Party did not win the election when he had just successfully led Britain to victory against Nazi Germany. He was also worried about whether the country would recover economically after the war. He thought the new socialist policies would cause vast and 'unnecessary' expenditure, which would have to be funded by heavier taxes on the middle and upper classes – traditional Conservative Party supporters. Nevertheless, it seemed the people of Britain wanted this change in society and the more equal opportunities of a **welfare state** that Labour had promised in their manifesto.

THE NEW

NATIONAL HEALTH SERVICE

*

Your new National Health Service begins on 5th July. What is it? How do you get it?

It will provide you with all medical, dental, and nursing care. Everyone—rich or poor, man, woman or child—can use it or any part of it. There are no charges, except for a few special items. There are no insurance qualifications. But it is not a "charity". You are all paying for it, mainly as taxpayers, and it will relieve your money worries in time of illness.

Leaflet issued to all British homes in 1948 outlining the new National Health Service

Establishing the welfare state

Attlee soon introduced a huge new range of **legislation** to start implementing the ideas proposed in the Labour manifesto. The 1946 National Health Service Act allowed everyone in the population, regardless of class or wealth, access to free medical and hospital treatment provided by the state. Average life expectancy increased by eight years, with free childhood vaccinations significantly reducing the infant mortality rate. The 1948 National Assistance Act ensured that those who were not in work, and therefore could not pay National Insurance, would still be provided for. Key industries such as coal, gas, iron, steel and electricity were **nationalised**, so that the government could provide secure employment and run them for the benefit of all rather than the profit of a few.

To deal with the housing shortage due to bomb damage during the war, the Labour government aimed to build 200 000 new houses per year. The 1947 Town and Country Planning Act required local councils to show how they were meeting this target, and the 1949 Housing Act controlled the amount of rent private landlords could charge tenants to prevent exploitation.

The welfare state was a transformation of the relationship between government and the people. There was now an expectation and understanding that the government should help to provide for its citizens. However, the issue of how to finance this huge increase in government spending became a key political issue for all following governments.

Check your understanding
1. What did William Beveridge identify as the main reasons for poverty?
2. How did Labour win the 1945 election?
3. In what ways did people's lives improve with the establishment of the welfare state?
4. How did the welfare state change the relationship between government and the people?
5. Why was the establishment of the welfare state met with criticism?

Unit 10: Postwar Britain
The postwar boom

The 1950s brought new prosperity to Britain and created much of what we now recognise as modern standards of living.

The Conservative governments from 1951 to 1963 introduced new economic measures to encourage people to spend more money on **consumer goods**. This fuelled a 'consumer boom'. With more people able to buy products and with the end of all rationing in 1954, companies started to utilise new technologies to create objects for the mass market. Factories that previously produced goods for war were adapted to suit the needs of peacetime, from cars, motorbikes and TVs to plastic furniture and children's toys. A range of new 'modern conveniences' also became available to make living spaces more comfortable, from central heating and vacuum cleaners to refrigerators, toasters, kettles and washing machines.

Advertising became commonplace, as people were encouraged to buy goods that many had only dreamed of before. By 1968 over 15 million households owned a TV compared to just 15 000 in 1947, and car ownership went up by 500 per cent between 1951 and 1964. The government also stepped in to improve infrastructure, such as the opening of the first motorway in 1958. Electricity and plumbing were also extended to more homes.

On 20 July 1957, Prime Minister **Harold Macmillan** made a speech declaring that with this new prosperity, Britain had "never had it so good". He became known as 'Supermac' for the rise in living standards people now enjoyed.

Radio and television advert in the UK's *Country Life* magazine, 1951

1951 Festival of Britain

This government-sponsored exhibition held on London's South Bank showcased new advancements in technology and modern designs and how they could be adapted into the home. Over 8.5 million people visited to celebrate and marvel at the technologies of the future.

Social liberation

During the 1960s, many groups of people gained new freedoms. The state began to withdraw from its role in censorship and harsh punishments to allow a '**permissive society**' to develop.

In education, the government intended to give more working-class children wider opportunities through the expansion of grammar schools and scholarships. In the 1960s, comprehensive schools were established to send all local children to a local school regardless of academic ability, and to mix boys and girls together in secondary education for the first time. The Open University was established in 1969, to promote higher education to wider groups of people who could distance-learn while working. In 1960, the obligation for young men to complete 18 months of National Service in the armed forces was ended, a change that coincided with the emergence of new forms of youth culture.

Despite their vital work in wartime, women had been expected to return to the traditional roles of housewife and mother, but new legislation began to give women more control of their own lives. The introduction of the contraceptive pill in 1961 and the legalisation of abortions in 1967 helped to prevent unwanted pregnancies. Divorce was made easier in 1969, enabling more women to leave unhappy marriages. Following women's strikes, like those of the sewing machinists at the Ford car factory in Dagenham, Labour MP Barbara Castle pushed through the Equal Pay Act of 1970. However, many inequalities persisted, from sexist advertising depicting women as unintelligent, sexual objects and housewives to domestic violence that often escalated to the murder of women. So in the 1970s, **feminist** activists founded the British women's liberation movement to continue campaigning for more change.

Women protesting for equal pay in Trafalgar Square, London, May 1969

There were also new strides forward in rights for LGBT+ people. The 1957 Wolfenden Report argued that the state should not intervene in people's private lives and therefore that homosexual relationships should not be punished. While homosexuality wasn't decriminalised until the Sexual Offences Act of 1967, the number of prosecutions began to fall. In 1970 the UK Gay Liberation Front was created and became a uniting force for change, just as the civil rights and feminist movements were.

During the postwar period, the media was also allowed to have more freedom in response to the changes happening in society. In 1960 the government took Penguin Books to court because they wanted to publish D. H. Lawrence's sexually explicit novel *Lady Chatterley's Lover,* which had been banned since 1928. The failure of the government to uphold the '**obscenity**' law in court allowed TV and films to include more violent and sexual scenes. These changes marked the beginning of the end of **deference** in the relationship between government and the media. Newspapers and television could now more openly mock politicians and challenge societal views.

In culture, as well as in commerce, it was clear that postwar Britain was going to be radically different to what came before.

British LGBT+ laws

LGBT+ people have existed throughout history and across the world. In 1533, Henry VIII was the first to make homosexuality illegal in Britain as a way to prosecute monks and accelerate the Dissolution of the Monasteries. Before this time, homosexuality was considered a religious rather than criminal matter.

Check your understanding

1. What types of new 'modern conveniences' became available in the 1950s?
2. How did the rise of consumer goods change people's lives in the 1950s?
3. How were people able to buy new consumer goods in the 1950s?
4. How did the lives of the working classes, women and LGBT+ people change during this period?
5. Why was the end of deference in the media significant?

Unit 10: Postwar Britain
Multicultural Britain

While there have always been people of different races and ethnicities living in Britain, the postwar period brought a larger number and wider range of people to Britain's shores than ever before.

After the Second World War, a larger workforce was needed to rebuild towns and cities that had been destroyed by German bombing. However, more than 2 million people decided to **emigrate** from Britain to **Commonwealth** countries such as Canada, Australia, New Zealand and South Africa. They wanted to leave behind the rationing, housing shortages and memories of war to enjoy better employment and new adventures abroad.

Commonwealth migration to Britain

As people left the UK, the British government became concerned about a labour shortage and aimed to recruit new White settlers. The 1948 British Nationality Act allowed anyone who was living in a Commonwealth country to re-settle in Britain as a British citizen. The government did not expect non-White settlers to arrive, but many people were excited to go to the 'mother country' of the British Empire that had been spoken about for generations. Furthermore, almost 3 million had even served in the armed forces to fight for Britain during the Second World War.

The term '**Windrush** generation' is used to describe the thousands of migrants from the Caribbean (then known as the West Indies) who came to Britain in the early postwar period. *Empire Windrush* was the most well-known ship to sail from Jamaica in 1948, carrying over 800 West Indians who intended to find work in Britain in response to the government's call for help. Thousands of Hindus, Sikhs and Muslims from India, Pakistan and Bangladesh also used their British passports to come to Britain in the postwar period.

Jamaicans arrive after travelling to London on *Empire Windrush*, June 1948

Race riots and tensions

Despite the fact that British citizens were coming to Britain to help with the postwar recovery, there was an undercurrent of racism in Britain that non-White **immigrants** had to face on their arrival. Not only were they often refused jobs for which they were qualified and paid less than White workers, it was also very hard to find housing, as landlords refused to rent to them.

In 1958, racism erupted into an outburst of violence against members of the non-White West London community in the Notting Hill race riots. Gangs of youths known as **Teddy Boys** were already causing antisocial behaviour across the country, and Black and Asian people soon became an easy target. This racial violence was emboldened by the rise of far-right groups such as the White Defence League, whose rallies fuelled anti-immigrant tensions. It became commonplace to find graffiti stating 'Keep Britain White'. Many pubs and dance halls refused entry to people of colour. In 1959 the first clear example of a racially motivated killing in London occurred when Kelso Cochrane was brutally murdered on his way home by a gang of White youths; none of the people responsible for his murder was brought to justice.

Protestors demonstrate in central London following the murder of Kelso Cochrane in 1959

'Rivers of Blood' speech

In 1968, Conservative MP Enoch Powell called for immigrants to be sent back to the countries of their birth. In a controversial speech he prophesised that if this did not happen there would be 'rivers of blood' as racial tensions would not be solved through integration. This revealed the structural racism at the heart of British attitudes towards immigration; surveys conducted at the time suggested that 74 per cent of the population supported his suggestion.

Government responses to racism

As the 1960s progressed, the civil rights struggle in the United States (see Unit 8, Chapters 3 and 4) became ever more relevant to the problems in Britain. Inspired by Rosa Parks, in 1963 Paul Stephenson led a boycott against the Bristol Omnibus Company who refused to employ Black or Asian people. In 1964, Malcolm X visited the West Midlands constituency of Smethwick where the Conservative candidate in the upcoming general election ran an overtly racist campaign.

Although the government passed Race Relations Acts in 1965 and 1968 to try to ban racial segregation in public places and racial discrimination within employment and housing, clear examples of racism within British society persisted. In 1968 the British Black Panthers were formed and in 1970 they led their most influential campaign at the trial of the 'Mangrove Nine' (see box).

In 1968 a highly controversial amendment to the Commonwealth Immigrants Act was pushed through parliament in just three days to remove the automatic right of migrants from the former British empire to settle in the UK, even if they held a valid British passport. Migrants now had to additionally prove a 'substantial personal connection' to Britain, such as a parent or grandparent born in the UK, which many migrants could not do.

The 'Mangrove Nine'

The 'Mangrove Nine' refers to nine Black activists who were arrested and put on trial in 1970 for 'inciting a riot' during a protest against unfair police raids on the Mangrove Caribbean restaurant in Notting Hill. The case quickly turned into an assessment of racism within the Metropolitan Police – why they had raided the restaurant in the first place? It led to the first acknowledgment of '**institutionalised racism**' in Britain.

Check your understanding
1. Why were British people emigrating abroad in 1945?
2. What was the purpose of the 1948 British Nationality Act?
3. What forms of racism did migrants suffer in the 1950s and 1960s?
4. In what ways did ethnic minorities fight against racism?
5. Why was the 1968 Commonwealth Immigrants Act controversial?

Margaret Thatcher

While the 1950s had seen a steady increase in living standards, by the late 1970s the postwar boom came to an end with a series of economic crises.

Governments struggled to deal with the rising costs of the welfare state, and millions of working days were being lost to **strike** action as **trade unions** campaigned for better wages. During the '**winter of discontent**' in 1978–9, bins went uncollected, coal was not mined, trains did not run and hospitals were closed – the country ground to a standstill. People began to argue that the unions were too powerful and that their strike action was damaging the UK economy.

The leader of the Conservative Party, Margaret Thatcher, had new ideas about how to deal with these problems in a radical way. In the general election in May 1979, Thatcher became Britain's first female Prime Minister.

Thatcher's economic revolution

Since 1945 both the Labour and Conservative parties had followed a policy of government intervention in the economy in order to run industries and maintain full employment. Thatcher believed this was causing inefficiency and that the government needed to step away from this role. Instead, she believed the **free market** should be allowed to operate without much regulation. This meant that some businesses would be allowed to decline in order for new ones to emerge. This marked the end of **consensus** between the parties over how to deal with the economy.

In practice, this meant that nationalised industries were sold off to private owners and **income tax** was cut to allow people to keep more of the wealth they earned. Thatcher believed that a desire for **profit** would motivate people to work harder and make businesses more efficient and competitive for fear of losing out to a competitor. There were opportunities for big profits in the financial sector with global businesses setting up offices in London. She also reduced the amount spent on the welfare state, as she believed it was creating a '**dependency culture**', with people relying on the state for jobs and benefits.

Margaret Thatcher (1925–2013), photographed in 1983

The 'Iron Lady'

First used in 1976 by a Soviet newspaper, Thatcher enjoyed this nickname as a demonstration of her firm stance on controversial issues. When she won the 1979 election, Thatcher was one of only 19 female MPs in the House of Commons – the other 616 were all men.

Thatcher on society

Thatcher had strong views against the liberal 'permissive society' of the 1960s and 1970s, and introduced new laws to curtail it. For example, Section 28 of the Local Government Act 1988 outlawed the 'promotion' of gay relationships in schools, which effectively meant teachers could not talk about gay people at all.

Breaking the power of the trade unions

Under Thatcher's new economic plans, the free market would close down unprofitable industries such as coal mining. Thatcher was determined to break the power of the trade unions and their leaders who disagreed with her policies.

With her position more secure after victory in the Falklands War and a landslide majority in the 1983 election, Thatcher announced that 20 coal pits would be closed with the loss of 20 000 jobs. No new forms of work would be provided to replace those lost. Thatcher knew that Arthur Scargill, the **militant** leader of the National Union of Miners, would immediately initiate strike action. So she had ensured that before this announcement was made, there was enough coal stockpiled to keep Britain going through the winter, even if the miners were not working. She also declared the strike illegal, meaning that the strikers were not entitled to benefits from the welfare state.

The miners' strikes went on for more than a year over 1984–5, with bitter and violent clashes between miners and police. Some miners decided to work through the strikes in order to still get paid, but were shunned by their communities. With reluctance, the miners eventually went back to work on low wages. The political and economic power of the unions had been broken and over the next seven years, 84 coal mines were closed down. The closure of these industries, without the establishment of new ones, meant that regional inequalities began to grow. Areas such as Yorkshire, Newcastle, Wales and Scotland faced unemployment and poverty, while cities in the south such as London became much wealthier.

In March 1990, riots broke out across the country in opposition to the introduction of a fixed 'poll tax' paid by every adult without regard for their income. Thatcher was eventually forced to resign in November 1990 by members of her own Party. Nevertheless, many of the changes she initiated during her time in power were maintained by subsequent governments. She remains the longest serving Prime Minister in modern British history.

The Falklands War

In 1982, unemployment figures continued to climb as Thatcher's free market economic theories were put to the test. The Argentinian invasion of the Falkland Islands in the South Atlantic Ocean provided an opportunity for her to portray herself as a determined leader, defending territories that had been deemed British Crown colonies since 1841. The war ended in a decisive victory for Britain.

Conflict between striking miners and police at the Orgreave Coking plant in Sheffield, South Yorkshire, during the miners' strike of 1984–5

Check your understanding

1. What happened during the 'winter of discontent'?
2. Why did Thatcher believe the free market was better than government intervention in the economy?
3. How did Thatcher break the power of the trade unions?
4. What impact did Thatcher's policies have on society?
5. Why is Thatcher seen as a divisive prime minister?

Unit 10: Postwar Britain
Britain and Europe

Throughout the postwar period, European countries that had previously spent centuries at war with each other began to move closer to an international union.

In 1957 the Treaty of Rome established the **European Economic Community** (**EEC**). This created a 'common market' that eliminated taxes on imports so that goods could be traded freely across the six nations of France, Luxembourg, Belgium, Italy, West Germany and the Netherlands. Free trade in goods meant that new jobs were created, incomes rose and prices fell. In the EEC's first decade, trade between the member states quadrupled.

As decolonisation was altering the British economy, it seemed that Europe would be the nearest trading partner and would be increasingly central to British trade. However, the French president **Charles de Gaulle** was deeply sceptical of Britain's applications to join the EEC. He knew that Britain still wanted to be an important world power, and was worried they would rival France for an unofficial leadership role within the EEC. Only when he was out of power did Britain join the EEC in 1973. The decision was confirmed in a **referendum** two years later, when 67 per cent of British voters voted to remain in the EEC.

In 1981 Greece joined the EEC, soon followed by Spain and Portugal in 1986. These southern European nations were significantly poorer and less industrialised than the other members of the EEC, so they benefited from economic aid and increased trade that the European system provided them.

Government pamphlets given to the British public ahead of the 1975 national referendum on the UK joining the EEC

The European Union

In 1992, the **Maastricht Treaty** officially created the **European Union** (**EU**). This was an extension of the EEC to create closer connections between the member states, and it called for common citizenship, currency and security policies. Part of the reason for the creation of the EU was the reunification of Germany following the fall of Communism (see Unit 7, Chapter 5). Some European leaders were fearful that Germany might again pose a threat to Europe. They felt that if each nation's prosperity depended on cooperation within a larger system, they would all work together harmoniously.

The EU pioneered greater integration between its member states. The 1985 **Schengen Agreement** allowed free, unrestricted movement of people to live, travel and work within almost all of the other member countries. Between 1999 and 2002 many member states chose to adopt a new currency called the Euro to make trade within the Union easier. In 2004 the former Soviet satellite states in Eastern Europe joined the EU. For nations still scarred by half a century of totalitarian rule, the support and funding provided by the EU was invaluable. The EU provided a framework of peaceful international movement, exchange and cooperation.

'Grexit'

Whether governments must follow referendum results is debatable. In 2015, a Greek referendum to leave the Eurozone had a 61 per cent majority, but the government ignored this to reach an agreement and stay.

Euroscepticism in Britain

Ever since the EEC was first established in 1957, there had been divisions over whether Britain should move closer to Europe or remain distant. Prominent politicians in both the Labour and Conservative parties were against joining the EEC. The referendum in 1975 was divisive, and feelings of '**euroscepticism**' within the parties remained.

Some people saw the EU as a threat to the **sovereignty** of nation states, taking decision making power away from their own government, and giving it to the European Commission – the governing body of the EU. The EU remained only partially democratic, with most of its leading officials appointed by governments rather than chosen by voters. Some people criticised the free movement of people, which they saw as giving up control of national borders. It was often argued that the arrival in Britain of workers from less well-off nations in Europe drove down wages for working class jobs. There were also concerns that the Maastricht Treaty in 1992 created more integration than the British voters had agreed to in the 1975 referendum.

Nigel Farage launches UKIP's EU referendum campaign ahead of a televised debate with British prime minister David Cameron, 7 June 2016

In 1993 the UK Independence Party (UKIP) was founded, and a politician named Nigel Farage became a leading voice in calls for Britain to break away from the European Union. In the 2010s the number of UKIP votes rose in local council elections, and the Conservative Party grew concerned that UKIP was drawing away Conservative voters. This led Conservative Prime Minister David Cameron to promise a referendum on Britain's membership of the EU in his manifesto for the 2015 election.

The referendum was held on 23 June 2016 and the results were very close. Overall, 52 per cent of voters chose to leave the European Union and 48 per cent of voters chose to remain (though when broken down by region, London, Scotland and Northern Ireland all voted to remain by clear majorities). 'Brexit', as it became known, became a major political issue in Britain as the parties and regions of the UK disagreed about how to manage a new relationship with Europe. The UK officially left the European Union on 31 January 2020 – the first member state to do so.

The United Kingdom's flag is taken down outside the European Parliament

Check your understanding

1. Why did it take Britain so long to join the European Economic Community (EEC)?
2. How was the European Union established in 1992?
3. What advantages did member nations hope to gain from European Union membership?
4. Why have people been Eurosceptic in Britain?
5. Why was the rise of the UK Independence Party significant?

Knowledge organiser

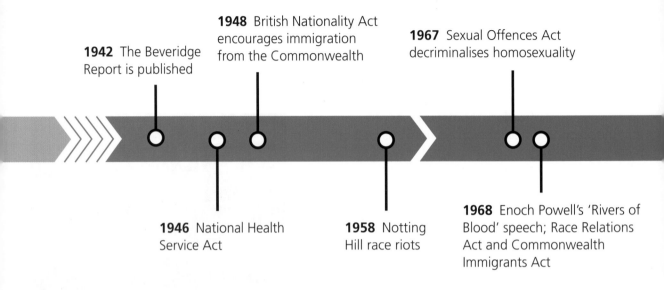

1942 The Beveridge Report is published

1948 British Nationality Act encourages immigration from the Commonwealth

1967 Sexual Offences Act decriminalises homosexuality

1946 National Health Service Act

1958 Notting Hill race riots

1968 Enoch Powell's 'Rivers of Blood' speech; Race Relations Act and Commonwealth Immigrants Act

Key vocabulary

Commonwealth Global association of 54 nations with links to the UK, founded in 1931; most members are former colonies of the British Empire, but all share equal status in the organisation

Consensus Agreement between different groups

Consumer goods Products made to be bought by customers

Deference Polite respect and submission to authority

Dependency culture A belief that too many people are given help by the welfare state

Emigrate To leave the country you were born in

European Economic Community (EEC) Economic union of European nations that evolved into the European Union

European Union(EU) Economic and political union of European nations

Euroscepticism Opposition to the EEC/EU

Feminist A person who supports women's equal rights with men

Free market An economic system of unrestricted competition between privately owned companies

General election A vote to elect the Members of Parliament for the House of Commons

Immigrant A person who lives in a country they were not born in

Income tax Tax taken by the government on the money you earn

Institutionalised racism Racism within official structures of a country such as government, the judiciary and the police

Legislation Laws passed by government

Maastricht Treaty Agreement that upgraded the EEC into the EU

Manifesto A declaration of the aims and goals of a pollical party in an election

Militant Adopting confrontational or violent methods of political protest

Nationalisation When the state takes control of an industry

Obscenity Words and ideas considered socially offensive/unacceptable

Permissive society A society where social norms become increasingly liberal; the term was used in the 1970s and 1980s to suggest this had resulted in a lowering of social standards

Profit The amount gained after costs have been deducted

Enquiry Question: Has postwar Britain made life fairer for more people?

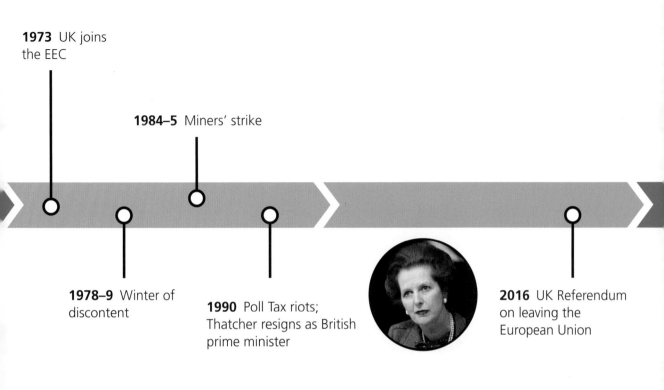

1973 UK joins the EEC

1984–5 Miners' strike

1978–9 Winter of discontent

1990 Poll Tax riots; Thatcher resigns as British prime minister

2016 UK Referendum on leaving the European Union

Key vocabulary

Prosperity Wealth

Referendum When the electorate are given a chance to vote on a particular political issue

Schengen Agreement Agreement that led to the abolition of most border checks between some EU countries to encourage free movement of people and goods

Socialist A person or policies promoting socialism

Sovereignty Authority of a state to govern itself

Strike Refusal to work as a form of protest

Teddy Boys Youth group of the 1950s with distinct style, often involved in violence

Trade union Formal organisation of workers in a specific industry

Welfare state A system where the government takes responsibility for the health and wellbeing of its citizens

Windrush Refers to the ship *Empire Windrush* and early migrants to Britain from the Caribbean (then known as the West Indies)

Winter of discontent The winter of 1978–9, characterised by severe strike action

Key people

Arthur Scargill Leader of the National Union of Miners from 1982 to 2002

Charles de Gaulle French president who refused Britain's entry into the EEC

Clement Attlee Labour Prime Minister 1945–51 who created the welfare state

Enoch Powell Conservative MP who gave the controversial 'Rivers of Blood' speech in 1968

Harold Macmillan Conservative Prime Minister 1957–63, during the postwar economic boom

Kelso Cochrane Victim of the first racially motivated killing in London in 1959

Margaret Thatcher Conservative Prime Minister 1979–90 and Britain's first female prime minister

Nigel Farage Leader of the UK Independence Party (UKIP) in 2006–9 and 2010–16

William Beveridge Economist who published an influential report on social reform in 1942

Timeline

1903 Emmeline Pankhurst establishes the WSPU

1912 The last Qing emperor abdicates

1914 (June) Assassination of Archduke Franz Ferdinand

1915 (January) First zeppelin air-raid in Britain

1915 (May) Sinking of the *Lusitania*

1916 (July) Battle of the Somme begins

1917 (February) A popular revolution overthrows the Tsar

1907 Formation of the Triple Entente

1913 Death of Emily Davison at the Epsom Derby

1914 (July) First World War begins

1915 (April) Gallipoli campaign begins

1916 (June) Arab Revolt begins

1917 The Balfour Declaration

1917 (April) USA enters the First World War

1942 (January) The Wannsee Conference

1942 'Quit India' resolution

1941 (June) Launch of Operation Barbarossa

1940 (September) The Blitz begins

1940 (June) Fall of France to the Germans and evacuation from Dunkirk

1939 (September) Children begin to be evacuated from cities

1939 (August) The Nazi–Soviet Pact

1942 The Beveridge Report is published

1941 (December) Japan attacks Pearl Harbor; USA enters Second World War

1940 Trotsky is assassinated in exile

1940 (July) Battle of Britain begins

1940 (May) Winston Churchill becomes Prime Minister of Britain

1939 (September) Germany invades Poland, beginning the Second World War

1938 (November) *Kristallnacht*

1942 (June) Battle of Midway begins US reconquest of the Pacific

1943 (February) Battle of Stalingrad ends in Soviet victory

1945 (May) Germany surrenders to the Allies

1945 (September) Japan surrenders to the Allies

1947 The USA adopts the Truman Doctrine

1948 British Nationality Act encourages immigration from the Commonwealth

1948 Foundation of the state of Israel

1942 (November) British victory at El Alamein gives the Allies the upper hand in North Africa

1944 (June) Allied reconquest of Europe begins with D-Day

1945 (August) USA drops atomic bombs on Hiroshima and Nagasaki.

1946 National Health Service Act

1947 India and Pakistan gain independence as separate nations

1948 Stalin begins the Berlin blockade

1949 NATO is formed

1990 Poll Tax riots; Thatcher resigns as British Prime Minister

1986 Chernobyl nuclear accident

1984–5 UK miner's strike

1976 Death of Mao Zedong

1973 US withdrawal from Vietnam

1991 Collapse of the Soviet Union

1998 The Good Friday Agreement

1989 Fall of Communism in the Soviet satellite states

1985 Mikhail Gorbachev comes to power in the USSR

1978–9 Winter of discontent

1973 UK joins the EEC

1972 US President Nixon visits China, opening China to relations with the West

2016 UK referendum on leaving the European Union

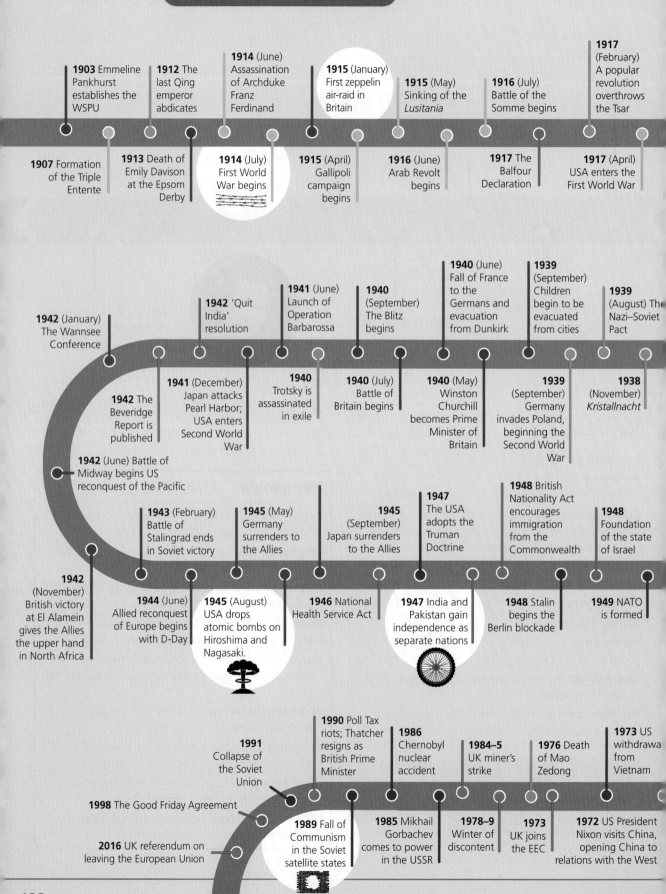

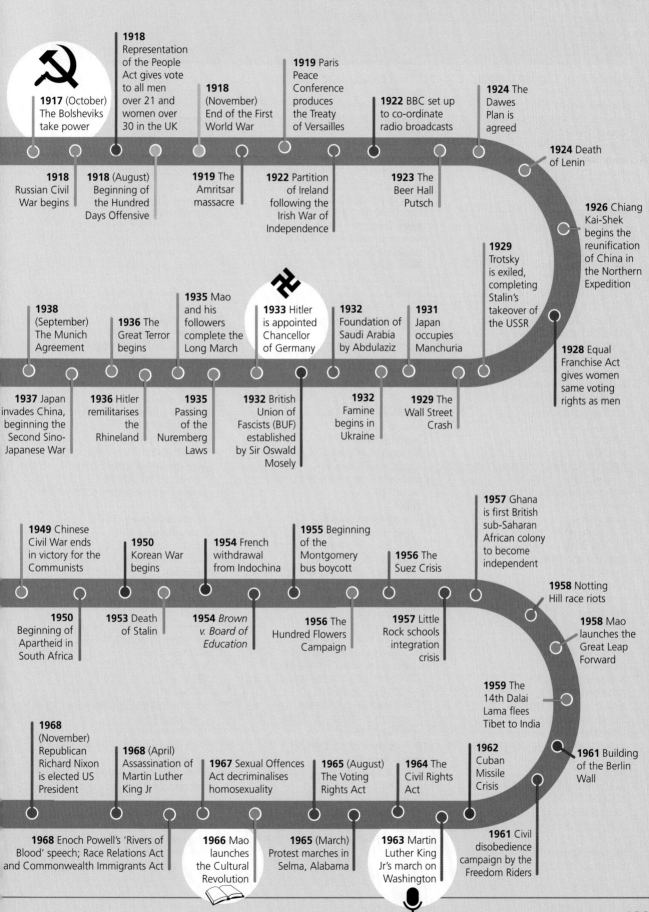

1917 (October) The Bolsheviks take power

1918 Representation of the People Act gives vote to all men over 21 and women over 30 in the UK

1918 Russian Civil War begins

1918 (August) Beginning of the Hundred Days Offensive

1918 (November) End of the First World War

1919 The Amritsar massacre

1919 Paris Peace Conference produces the Treaty of Versailles

1922 Partition of Ireland following the Irish War of Independence

1922 BBC set up to co-ordinate radio broadcasts

1923 The Beer Hall Putsch

1924 The Dawes Plan is agreed

1924 Death of Lenin

1926 Chiang Kai-Shek begins the reunification of China in the Northern Expedition

1928 Equal Franchise Act gives women same voting rights as men

1929 Trotsky is exiled, completing Stalin's takeover of the USSR

1929 The Wall Street Crash

1931 Japan occupies Manchuria

1932 Foundation of Saudi Arabia by Abdulaziz

1932 Famine begins in Ukraine

1933 Hitler is appointed Chancellor of Germany

1932 British Union of Fascists (BUF) established by Sir Oswald Mosely

1935 Mao and his followers complete the Long March

1935 Passing of the Nuremberg Laws

1936 The Great Terror begins

1936 Hitler remilitarises the Rhineland

1938 (September) The Munich Agreement

1937 Japan invades China, beginning the Second Sino-Japanese War

1949 Chinese Civil War ends in victory for the Communists

1950 Beginning of Apartheid in South Africa

1950 Korean War begins

1953 Death of Stalin

1954 French withdrawal from Indochina

1954 *Brown v. Board of Education*

1955 Beginning of the Montgomery bus boycott

1956 The Hundred Flowers Campaign

1956 The Suez Crisis

1957 Little Rock schools integration crisis

1957 Ghana is first British sub-Saharan African colony to become independent

1958 Notting Hill race riots

1958 Mao launches the Great Leap Forward

1959 The 14th Dalai Lama flees Tibet to India

1961 Building of the Berlin Wall

1961 Civil disobedience campaign by the Freedom Riders

1962 Cuban Missile Crisis

1968 (November) Republican Richard Nixon is elected US President

1968 (April) Assassination of Martin Luther King Jr

1967 Sexual Offences Act decriminalises homosexuality

1965 (August) The Voting Rights Act

1964 The Civil Rights Act

1968 Enoch Powell's 'Rivers of Blood' speech; Race Relations Act and Commonwealth Immigrants Act

1966 Mao launches the Cultural Revolution

1965 (March) Protest marches in Selma, Alabama

1963 Martin Luther King Jr's march on Washington

Index

Acknowledgements

Every effort has been made to trace copyright holders and to obtain their permission for use of copyright material. The publishers will gladly receive any information enabling them to rectify any error or omission at first opportunity. The publishers would like to thank the following for permission to reproduce copyright material:

(t = top, b = bottom, c = centre, l = left, r = right)

cover Pictorial Press Ltd / Alamy Stock Photo, p8 Everett Collection/Shutterstock, p9t Pictorial Press Ltd/Alamy Stock Photo, p9b Collins Bartholomew Ltd, p10 Collins Bartholomew Ltd, p11 GL Archive/Alamy Stock Photo, p12t and 18 Everett Collection/Shutterstock, p12b IanDagnall Computing / Alamy Stock Photo, p13 Granger, NYC. / Alamy Stock Photo, p14 Everett Collection/Shutterstock, p15t CBW / Alamy Stock Photo, p15b GL Archive / Alamy Stock Photo, p16t Everett Collection/Shutterstock, p16b Everett Collection/Shutterstock, p20 Hazel McAllister / Alamy Stock Photo, p21t Everett Collection/Shutterstock, p21b Shutterstock/Oleg Golovnev, p22 Pictorial Press / Alamy Stock Photo, p23t Shutterstock/Everett Collection, p23b David Cole / Alamy Stock Photo, p24 Pictorial Press / Alamy Stock Photo, p25t Everett Collection/Shutterstock, p25b and 31 AF archive / Alamy Stock Photo, p26 Sueddeutsche Zeitung Photo / Alamy Stock Photo, p27 Artyom Smirnova / Alamy Stock Photo, p28 Igors / Alamy Stock Photo, p28 World of Triss / Alamy Stock Photo, p29 IgorGolovniov/Shutterstock, p32 Everett Collection/Shutterstock, p33t Pictorial Press Ltd / Alamy Stock Photo, p33b Arterra Picture Library / Alamy Stock Photo, p34t Everett Collection/Shutterstock, p34b INTERFOTO / History / Alamy Stock Photo, p35 Süddeutsche Zeitung Photo / Alamy Stock Photo, p36b Everett Collection/Shutterstock, p36r Chronicle / Alamy Stock Photo, p37t Everett Collection/Shutterstock, p38 dpa picture alliance / Alamy Stock Photo, p39t World History Archive / Alamy Stock Photo, p39b Arterra Picture Library / Alamy Stock Photo, p40 Everett Collection / Alamy Stock Photo, p41t Shawshots / Alamy Stock Photo, p41b Everett Collection/Shutterstock, p44 Everett Collection/Shutterstock, p45 akg-images / Alamy Stock Photo, p46 Everett Collection/Shutterstock, p47 US National Archives / Alamy Stock Photo, p48 World History Archive / Alamy Stock Photo, p49t David Ball / Alamy Stock Photo, p49b Pictorial Press Ltd / Alamy Stock Photo, p50 Everett Historical/Shutterstock, p51t Shutterstock/Yeongsik Im, p51b Pictorial Press / Alamy Stock Photo, p52 Heritage Image Partnership Ltd/ Alamy Stock Photo, p53t Everett Collection/Shutterstock, p53c Pictorial Press Ltd / Alamy Stock Photo, p56 Chronicle / Alamy Stock Photo, p57 INTERFOTO / Alamy Stock Photo, p58 De Luan / Alamy Stock Photo, p59 Colin Waters / Alamy Stock Photo, p60 Bond Smith Family Archive / Alamy Stock Photo, p61 Shawshots / Alamy Stock Photo, p62 Pictorial Press Ltd / Alamy Stock Photo, p63 Everett Collection Historical / Alamy Stock Photo ,p64 Shawshots / Alamy Stock Photo, p65t Everett Historical/Shutterstock, p65c Shawshots / Alamy Stock Photo, p68 Shutterstock/Everett Collection, p69 Photo 12 / Alamy Stock Photo ,p70 Scherl/Süddeutsche Zeitung Photo / Alamy Stock Photo, p71t mccool / Alamy Stock Photo, p71b Shutterstock/Everett Collection, p72 INTERFOTO / History / Alamy Stock Photo, p73t Everett Collection / Alamy Stock Photo, p73b Science History Images / Alamy Stock Photo, p74 Everett Collection / Alamy Stock Photo, p75 CPA Media Pte Ltd / Alamy Stock Photo, p76 Glasshouse Images / Alamy Stock Photo, p77b Dennis Brack / DanitaDelimont / Alamy Stock Photo, p80 GL Archive / Alamy Stock Photo, p81 Joshua Davenport/Shutterstock, p82 Maps © Collins Bartholomew Limited 2019, p83 Everett Historical/Shutterstock, p84 Everett Collection/Shutterstock, p85 World History Archive / Alamy Stock Photo, p86 World History Archive / Alamy Stock Photo, p87 Granger Historical Picture Archive / Alamy Stock Photo, p88 Shutterstock/Heide Pinkall, p89t ITAR-TASS News Agency / Alamy Stock Photo, p89b Agencja Fotograficzna Caro / Alamy Stock Photo, p92c GL Archive / Alamy Stock Photo, p92b Everett Collection/Shutterstock, p94 Everett Collection/Shutterstock, p95t Everett Collection/Shutterstock, p95c Everett Collection Inc / Alamy Stock Photo, p96t and 102 (spot image) Granger Historical Picture Archive / Alamy Stock Photo, p96b Everett Collection Inc / Alamy Stock Photo, p97 Everett Collection Historical / Alamy Stock Photo, p98l Everett Collection Historical / Alamy Stock Photo, p98r Everett Collection Historical / Alamy Stock Photo, p99t Pictorial Press Ltd / Alamy Stock Photo, p99b Everett Collection/Shutterstock, p100 Everett Collection Inc / Alamy Stock Photo, p101 Granger Historical Picture Archive / Alamy Stock Photo, p105t Joaquin Ossorio Castillo/Shutterstock, p105b VanderWolf Images/Shutterstock, p106 Everett Collection Inc / Alamy Stock Photo, p107 Pictures From History / Alamy Stock Photo, p108 Matthew Corrigan / Alamy Stock Photo, p109 UtCon Collection / Alamy Stock Photo, p110 Pictorial Press Ltd / Alamy Stock Photo, p111 Keystone Press / Alamy Stock Photo, p112 Everett Collection / Alamy Stock Photo, p112 Tom Wurl/Shutterstock, p114 History collection 2016 / Alamy Stock Photo, p115 World History Archive / Alamy Stock Photo, p116 RKive / Alamy Stock Photo, p117 Trinity Mirror / Mirrorpix / Alamy Stock Photo, p118 PA / Alamy Stock Photo, p119 KEYSTONE Pictures USA / Alamy Stock Photo, p120 Homer Sykes / Alamy Stock Photo, p121 Trevor Smith / Alamy Stock Photo, p122 Terry Mathews / Alamy Stock Photo, p123 Lee Thomas / Alamy Stock Photo, p123 ALEXANDROS MICHAILIDIS / Alamy Stock Photo